Not So Sweet

Sixteen Plays from
Soho Rep's Ten-Minute Festival

NOT SO SWEET

*Sixteen Plays from
Soho Rep's Ten-Minute Festival*

Edited by
Daniel Aukin
Artistic Director, Soho Repertory Theatre

GARDEN CITY, NEW YORK

Acknowledgements

The editor would like to thank Lisa Burdige and Emily Jenkins for suggesting the project and for executing the huge amount of legwork involved; John Guare, for recommending I add the interviews; Theron Albis for introducing the book to my editor Mark Glubke at Bookspan; Jamie Wolf, for legal assistance; the co-producer of Summer Camp 4, Simon Hammerstein; the producers of Summer Camp 5, Linsay Firman and Stephen Rahe; the producers of Summer Camp 3, David Levine and Dan Dzindzihashvili for getting me into this mess; the many interns and volunteers who make the Summer Camp series happen every year, a seemingly never-ending miracle; the directors, actors, and crews who worked on each ten-minute play when it was performed at Soho Rep; the staff of Soho Repertory Theatre, in particular Bridget Markov and Alexandra Conley; and Paul Sahre, Soho Rep's graphic designer, for inspiring the book jacket.

Contents

Editor's Note

I have a confession. I love theater. I also spend a lot of time and energy witnessing, complaining about, and generally bemoaning this thing that I love, this calling, this beast with too many heads. Why do it? Too often, working in a theater which develops new plays feels like facing an army of people shouting "No." The battles are many, and most at a fierce incline.

Then, sometimes unexpectedly, I hear a resounding *Yes*. It might be a great performance, or an astonishing piece of playwriting or an odd, sideways silence before a character speaks. Whatever it is, it thrills me something stupid, feeding a hunger I did not know I had, and before I know it I'm writing imaginary manifestos and planning hugely ambitious projects. For as long as the *Yes* lasts, the *Nos* melt away and the thought of doing anything else is revealed to be the patently absurd delusion it always was.

As Artistic Director of Soho Rep, I head an organization dedicated to the development of new plays. We present two or three large Mainstage productions every season—plays that run for at least five weeks and which are regularly reviewed by the major New York City press. The development of new plays, however, is the keystone of our activity. At the heart of Soho Rep's play-development philosophy is the idea that plays are best developed through production. With our development series, Summer Camp and R&D: Research & Development, we provide a forum for the debate about the future of our medium in an atmosphere of collaboration and discussion. The productions mounted during our developmental programs are experiments. The artists involved work in an atmosphere of healthy, supportive risk-taking. Professional critics are excluded from these workshops in order to protect both the artists and their work in their infancy, and to preserve the future life of the plays and their productions.

This collection, a selection of sixteen ten-minute plays from Summer Camp 3 and Summer Camp 4, is about that moment of saying *Yes*. The material, both in form and content, ranges wildly from the naturalistic, to the socially conscious, to the formally experimental. While the final results cover a huge expanse of dramatic territory, each of these new voices is in some way engaged with the struggle of writing for the theater today. For the theater to continue to be a culturally dynamic field, each new generation of artists has to find its own special way through the struggle, to make it their own (I wish that sounded less pat, but there you go). I hope you will share my excitement for the singularly angled passion each of these young playwrights directs at the stage.

My first experience with Soho Rep was as a writer. I considered and still do consider myself a director first and foremost. But I had written one full-length play and when the producers of the Summer Camp 3 asked me to contribute a ten-minute play, I recklessly obliged. The following year I co-produced Summer Camp 4 and soon after I became Soho Rep's Artistic Director. Summer Camp is extremely dear to my heart, for the opportunity it gave me and for the opportunities it continues to create, year after delirious year.

Some More Details About the Book

Although short, a ten-minute play is still that—a play. These bite-size nuggets of theater prove that depth comes from something besides length. They unfold complete and rich worlds in the space of a coffee break. Evenings of ten-minute plays are full of energy and increasing in popularity. Across the country, venues like Actor's Theater of Louisville, Todo Con Nada, Cleveland Public Theater, and The Ontological have been launching ten-minute festivals as a way of reaching new audiences. The ten-minute might even be called a post-modern dramatic form.

For the past four years, the Soho Rep Ten-Minute Festival has sold out every performance. While ten-minute plays appeal to the short attention-span, TV junkie audience, I contend that *Not So Sweet* and the Soho Rep festival use the form for a higher purpose. They showcase young playwrights—innovative artists who are expanding and developing American theater.

These sixteen playwrights represent the next wave of the daring writers who have been Soho Rep's hallmark in the downtown New York theater scene since 1975. They test the limits of language, searching for new voices in which to speak and new ways to stage their ideas, yet they never forget the storytelling that is essential to the theater. Their work inhabits that rare space where accessibility meets bold theatricality.

Voices from the Sexual Sidelines

Sexual identity is shaped by psychoanalysis, by schooling, by social strictures, and by language. These five plays take erotic anxieties and desires as their starting points, and explore the construction of the sexual self through language. Here are voices that include sexually abusive rants, erotic fantasies of domination and submission, voyeuristic pleasures, and the emerging awareness of sexuality.

Lisa Burdige's *The Tutors* shows a pair of college writing students becoming victims of the scholastic lingo and sadistic sexual fantasies of their English tutors. It exposes the eroticism inherent yet forbidden in the teacher-pupil relationship. In *No Evil*, Emily Jenkins follows three adolescent girls into their secret hideout, where they act out their fears and lusts while discussing bruises, growing breasts, junior-high politics, rabbit turds, and mountains of candy. Their verbal strategies keep the evils of the outside world at bay. In *The Metropolitan*, Mark Green has artfully demonstrated how the street-tough talk of a pair of Brooklyn homeboys conceals—and eventually reveals—a wrenching admission of sexuality. *Cyclone of Rage*, by David Lindsay-Abaire, takes the eroticized environment of the psychoanalyst's office to newly hysterical and insightful extremes. When a madwoman demands a Freudian shrink show his true colors, his (and her) duplicities and hypocrisies are exposed. And in Dennis Davis's *Oedipus Retched!* the classic story of father, mother, and son gets reimagined and demythified through the voice of a modern-day storyteller. The sexual tragedy comes alive in the present day, just the twisted story of a dirty riddler and the dysfunctional family history he predicted.

Voices of the Urban Sprawl

The urban environment is a self-constructed jungle whose inhabitants live and speak a unique and constantly shifting language. The six plays in this section show the body and mind affected by the polymorphous city—Italian-Americans in a tight-knit community, African-American teenagers longing to escape their literal and literary ghetto, night wanderers on a Montreal bus. The rhythms and the structures of the city are like a magnifying glass, making cultural differences and personal idiosyncracies loom enormous as people negotiate the cramped, over-stimulating world they inhabit.

John Poglinco's two plays depict singularly urban rhythms of Italian-American speech that are both instantly recognizably and utterly unique. In *Over Here*, Catholic Mass inhibits and re-directs the conversation of two long-time friends and sometime enemies. During the service, they run down the hierarchy of their community as they sort out their troubles. In *Macchinista*, a pair of fanciful Italian-American mechanics begin discussing the tools of their trade and find themselves contemplating being and non-being, philosophy and religion. Shop talk becomes a matter of life and death. In my own *Saucy Paper*, a tourist in a European cafe taps into her previously unknown identity as an agent scheduled to subvert the insidious mind-control operations of an all-powerful bureaucracy. The strange, temporary position of tourists in a foreign city works as a metaphor for the condition of the human mind in the corporate world . . . or something like that. In *Icebox*, by J.R. Riddick, the conversations of pair of teenage boys playing skelley in a Brooklyn neighborhood intersect with the poetic ramblings of a crazy woman sitting on the stoop nearby. The boys play with language and create shifting versions of themselves, strategies to deal with the love and anger they feel towards her. *True Confessions* by Dan Dzindzihashvili portrays apartment-living at its most poignant and painful. An elderly man spends an evening in a decrepit hallway, wearing only his underwear. His excuses, lies, explanations, and pleadings are directed at someone on the other side of the door. And Madelyn Kent's *Crawl* finds two passengers on a Montreal bus. The public space suddenly becomes a place for intimacies as their bodies, his smelling of excrement and sweat, hers bleeding from a botched home abortion, move through a threatening city, protected by the hard metal bus.

Voices Within Conflicted Families

Charged with the present and future dreams of its members, the family is always faced with the unspoken drama of being both what it is and what is should be—simultaneously. The plays in this section explore the family paradox: the claustrophobia of closeness and loneliness of familiarity. These characters are constantly struggling with who their families want them to be, who their families make them, and who they wish they could become. In *Confessions, Bedside*, by Jason T. Garrett, the language of love gets translated into the language of satire as a homosexual couple finds that, without the traditional family structure, they are at a loss for how to grieve over one partner's imminent death. Witty, bitter, and shameless, their dialogue evades the issues and yet communicates the truth. Funny and unexpected, Henry Kandel's *Gazelle* deconstructs the modern norms for father-son relationships and the unspoken gender typing that erodes them. When a great little league batter and his feminist coach reveal their goddess-worship, the boy's father finds his pride shriveling. There's a little "pansy" in the best of hitters. In *Dinner*, a young woman brings her current sexual fascinations into her upper-class home. Lucy Thurber's punchy dialogue rips open classism, racism, myopia, and sexual implications of family life—while posing the question: how do we recognize our kin? *Clock*, Neena Beber's hypothetical family drama, elongates a single moment. As a father and daughter struggle to connect, time seems to fold. Memory, presence, and possibility intersect. And in *The Friendly Neighborhood*, by Michael Chung, the love-hate dynamic of the family is acted out through the extreme mannerisms of commedia dell'arte clowns. The supposedly happy families of situation comedies are (literally) ripped to shreds, revealing underlying rage and violence.

DANIEL AUKIN
Artistic Director, Soho Rep
September 4, 2000

Not So Sweet

Sixteen Plays from
Soho Rep's Ten-Minute Festival

Voices from the Sexual Sidelines

So's, more sooners than laters, Eddie meets up with this other cat, Griphon Jones, who actually is this cat thing, come sphincter monster, and oh so, so much, more. And Griphon's running this protection racket, on this one town, Thebes. So's, Eddie's like, cool, I'm no fool, not my problem, not my business, just let me pass. And Griphon's like, pass my ass, here's a riddle, what's green and smells like pork?

—Dennis Davis, *Oedipus Retched!*

ELSIE: Oh, Lace, don't ever wear the underwires. I read they cut off the circulation to your boobs and make them atrophy.

LACIE: I don't even want to know what that means.

ELSIE: It means they turn black and fall off.

TILLIE: No, no. It means they get all skinny and can't do their job properly. My uncle's arm got atrophied after he had it in a cast.

ELSIE: That's gotta be wrong. How could boobies get skinny and not do their job properly?

TILLIE: They could.

—Emily Jenkins, *No Evil*

THE TUTORS   *by Lisa Burdige*

Characters:

Tutor One: A young man or woman in his or her mid-twenties.

Tutor Two: A young woman, slightly younger than Tutor One.

Student One: A hulking, eighteen-year-old college football player. He is dressed in athletic clothing as if he is on his way to practice.

Student Two: A moderately attractive eighteen-year-old girl with a slightly bovine gaze.

Policeman: A young man in his mid-twenties. He should be well-built, and strikingly handsome.

Setting: The Learning Center of a second-class university. The stage is divided in half to suggest two cubicles or offices.

At rise: Tutor One sits behind a large gray institutional desk. Several books including a dictionary, a thesaurus, and a grammar handbook are stacked on the desk. Tutor Two is sitting behind a large round table staring at a clock hanging center stage. Student One, wearing a varsity football letter jacket, stands outside an imaginary door waiting. He holds a paper obviously marked up with red ink.)

TUTOR ONE (*while masturbating*): Teachers are like parents, they are not supposed to fuck. If we fuck then we are no longer authority figures. We become unclean. Unfit to shape little minds. Or in our case, not so little minds—which makes it even worse. What would happen if I went to a bar and picked up a fine young thing, took that piece of sumptuous flesh home and fucked its brains out? What would happen if that beautiful but stupid specimen showed up in my class? How would I concentrate? How could I give a grade without thinking about the body, the gyrating body? The bodily fluids. The flickering wordless tongue so much more effective uttering meaningless syllables.

(*A knock at the door. Tutor One orgasms*)

TUTOR ONE (*moaning*): One . . . minute.

STUDENT ONE: I have to come in. I have football practice in a half an hour. You have to sign my paper or else I'll fail my course.

TUTOR TWO: A teacher is just like a vampire, sucking on words and desiring flesh. I hate this place.

TUTOR ONE: Freud said that academics could not fuck if they wanted to do their work. Freud said that creative writers need to fuck in order to do their work.

TUTOR TWO: I want to be a writer. Not a writer of marginalia, but a writer of great thoughts and emotion. I want to suck in sex and spit out beauty—sound and color. Images.

TUTOR ONE: Freud said teachers cannot fuck.

TUTOR TWO: I never wanted to be a teacher. I wanted to be a writer.

STUDENT ONE (*knocking on imaginary door*): Can I come in?

TUTOR TWO: I am never too happy to leave this place. When I get in my car, I am in a frenzy to escape, to move towards something more tangible than words shaped like a keyhole. I rush out quickly, running all the red lights until I get to the highway and I can see the harbor, a shoreline of polluted beaches dotted with low, squat oil containers. I should have worked on an oil rig or become a plumber.

(*Enter Student Two*)

STUDENT TWO (*to Student One*): Are you waiting?

STUDENT ONE: Yes I'm waiting. You must be very stupid.

STUDENT TWO: I am very stupid. Which is why I hope we won't have to wait too long. I need a lot of tutoring.

STUDENT ONE: I'm late for football practice.

STUDENT TWO: I'm so stupid that I'm impressed. (*Pauses*) I guess you're a football player.

TUTOR ONE: You can come in now.

(*Student One enters cubicle and sits in chair next to Tutor One's desk. He takes out his books while Tutor Two speaks*)

TUTOR TWO: "In the beginning," "thus," "in conclusion" . . . I get nauseous sucking on so many words. I need air—I need flesh. I run the red lights and I don't care if I get caught.

STUDENT ONE (*reading from papers*): "It must have been the rat sandwiches they fed us in the cafeteria, because when I got out into the woods I had to take a big dump."

TUTOR ONE: Is that an important detail?

STUDENT ONE: It's crucial to the story.

TUTOR ONE: Okay good. But there's a problem with your diction.

STUDENT ONE: Hey keep my diction out of this. You know I'm late for football practice.

TUTOR ONE: Can you think of another way of writing big dump?

STUDENT ONE: Big shit.

TUTOR ONE: Better.

(*They freeze*)

TUTOR TWO: Yesterday after class I ran the red light outside the faculty parking lot. Then I sped down past the Merit station, took the curve under the highway way too fast, and ran another the light in front of the Pompei Pizzeria. When I heard the siren I wondered if I got a ticket would I lose my job? Teachers aren't supposed to speed. The policeman asked me to get out of the car.

(*Enter Policeman wearing black leather boots and mirrored "CHIPS" sunglasses*)

POLICEMAN: You wore that outfit while you were in graduate school . . . .

TUTOR TWO: Am I getting a ticket for speeding?

POLICEMAN (*getting down on his knees and massaging Tutor Two's thighs*): You used to wear that outfit to academic conferences and cock-tail parties and Ph.D. seminars. Even then it was a little Madonnaesque. When you crossed your legs in class everybody could see the lacey line of your black garter belt and wonder if you were wearing underwear. I'm wondering if you're wearing underwear.

TUTOR TWO: I'm not. Am I getting a ticket for going too slowly?

POLICEMAN (*kissing her between the legs*): For treading water really.

TUTOR TWO: Nice use of imagery. If I give you a blow job will you put away that pencil and ticket pad?

(*Student Two knocks on imaginary door. They freeze. Policeman rises and exits*)

STUDENT TWO: Can I come in?

TUTOR TWO (*waving good-bye to exiting Policeman*): Now he has lovely flesh.

STUDENT TWO: Can I come in?

(*Student Two enters, sits in chair opposite Tutor Two. She leans over tables as if to ask Tutor Two a question. They freeze. Tutor One and Student One unfreeze*)

TUTOR ONE: How about feces?

STUDENT ONE (*writing as he rereads the sentence*): It must have been the rat sandwiches they fed us in the cafeteria, because when I got out into the woods I had to take a big feces.

TUTOR ONE: Feces is misused. Wrong word.

STUDENT ONE: But you told me to use it.

TUTOR ONE: I may have mentioned it while we were brainstorming, but I never said it would work.

(*Tutor One and Student One freeze. Student Two and Tutor Two unfreeze*)

STUDENT TWO: I'm sorry that I'm stupid.

TUTOR TWO: Rule number one: never state the obvious.

STUDENT TWO: But it's true.

TUTOR TWO: Rule number two: nobody cares about the truth. Your purpose here has nothing to do with the truth. You are here to learn how to write an effective five-paragraph essay.

STUDENT TWO: I guess the truth isn't very effective.

TUTOR TWO: You're stating the obvious again.

(*Enter Policeman. Student Two freezes*)

POLICEMAN (*to Tutor Two*): If you need me to write any tickets just let me know.

TUTOR TWO: Thanks. But it's not pedagogically sound to use words when you communicate with students. They only understand letters.

POLICEMAN: How about a fine? That's a number.

TUTOR TWO: I'm afraid the math lab might get upset. They might feel threatened. We don't want to get mixed up in university politics.

(*Exit Policeman. Tutor One and Tutor Two unfreeze*)

TUTOR ONE: Nice backup.

TUTOR TWO: Thanks.

STUDENT ONE (*shaking out his muscles*): This is harder than football practice. I don't know what to do. Teach me.

TUTOR ONE: I can't teach you how to write. I can only help you to learn for yourself. Here look up "big dump" in the thesaurus.

(*Tutor One freezes. Student One continues to flip through thesaurus*)

TUTOR ONE (*without moving*): Freeze.

(*Student One groans and then unwillingly freezes*)

STUDENT TWO: I don't even know where to begin.

TUTOR TWO: What are you writing about?

STUDENT TWO: Okay. My teacher wants me to write about an important person, place, or thing that has helped or hindered me in the past, future, or present. I'm supposed to use narrative, comparison and contrast, classification, inductive and deductive reasoning, and a lot of descriptive language.

TUTOR TWO: An excellent prompt. (*To Tutor One*) Did you hear that writing prompt?

TUTOR ONE: I think I wrote that writing prompt.

STUDENT TWO: Well, you are my teacher.

TUTOR ONE: Then I guess I did write it.

STUDENT ONE (*unfreezing and slamming thesaurus down*): Here. "Big dump" means to put many things in one place.

TUTOR ONE: That's a definition. And anyway, it doesn't help.

STUDENT ONE: Maybe I should look "shit" up in the thesaurus.

TUTOR ONE: You see, you're learning already.

STUDENT ONE: Good, because I have to go to football practice. Can you write a note to my teacher so I don't fail?

TUTOR ONE: Certainly, I will be happy to write a note, I wrote my Doctoral Thesis on the pre, during, and after effects of writing notes for students heavily invested in athletics. And I'll have you know it was published. (*While writing*) Dear Teacher. We discussed the major details in the student's paper. He was able to understand the concept of brainstorming and using the thesaurus and transfer his knowledge into a tangible first line.

STUDENT ONE: Did you sign it?

TUTOR ONE: Of course I did.

STUDENT ONE: Thanks.

(*Student One exits shaking out his muscles as he walks. Tutor One puts a "Do Not Disturb" sign on desk and turns back to audience*)

TUTOR TWO: So what are you going to write about?

STUDENT TWO: My mother. She stripped and turned tricks at Runway 69. We used to live behind the club.

TUTOR TWO: Madonna-whore—it's a cliché.

STUDENT TWO: But it's true, and besides I don't know what else to write about.

TUTOR TWO: It's a cliché. (*Calling out to Tutor One*) Isn't it a cliché?

TUTOR ONE (*unbuttoning shirt*): Teachers, like parents, shouldn't fuck. Freud said the Madonna-whore was an archetype not a person.

TUTOR TWO: And you see, it's a cardinal sin. You just can't write about your mother's sexuality. We have a collective morality. It's not that we're censoring you, we just know the kind of subject that makes a good essay.

STUDENT TWO: But I have a thesis statement. (*Reading from paper*) My mother loved me.

TUTOR TWO: Now, that's really a cliché.

TUTOR ONE: Have her brainstorm.

TUTOR TWO: What's the point? The topic is . . .

TUTOR ONE (*interrupting and with a sense of urgency*): Have her brainstorm! (*Motions to the policeman to come closer. To Policeman*) Tell her.

POLICEMAN: I'm sorry Miss, I'm going to have to ask you to cooperate with the gentleman.

TUTOR ONE: Have her describe someone, someone associated with her mother.

TUTOR TWO: Like her father?

STUDENT TWO: My mother said my father was Tom, Dick, and Harry.

TUTOR TWO: Anybody can be Tom, Dick, and Harry. Use specific language. Narrow your topic.

(*Student Two talks while Tutor One masturbates*)

STUDENT TWO: Tom had light blond, curly hair. Dick was black, I mean really black. He had an afro and wore those African robes when he wasn't in his g-string. Harry was pretty young, I guess he was about my age now. He was Filipino, I think. My mother said his penis curved up like a hook or a question mark.

TUTOR ONE (*moaning slightly*): Nice detail.

(*Enter Policeman. He begins an erotic dance which leads to a striptease in front of Tutor Two. Student Two continues to speak and does not notice*)

STUDENT TWO: I liked Dick the best, he used to bring me chocolate chip cookies. Sometimes we'd even bake them in the kitchen of the club. They'd always taste like chicken wings because that's all the club served. Spicy buffalo chicken wings. Did you ever try chocolate chip cookies with hot sauce? That was Dick's specialty.

(*Policeman strips down to his boxers and begins undulating. Tutor Two exits cubicle to stage left. She gets down on her knees and follows the movements of the policeman's pelvis with her hands*)

TUTOR TWO (*moaning*): Flesh.

TUTOR ONE: Yes, more flesh.

STUDENT TWO: Okay. Dick had firm flesh. When he flexed his arms you could see his biceps and triceps dance. Harry, too. Although his skin was lighter. They were *like* chocolate chip cookies. Harry the cookie part and Dick the chips. Which makes Tom the milk, I guess.

I never thought of that. Isn't that what you call a metaphor or something?

(*Tutor Two and Policeman begin to pantomime fucking*)

TUTOR TWO (*between thrusts*): We're not evaluating right now. We're just expressing ourselves.

STUDENT TWO: I loved Harry's hair. It was black—fine and shiny and so straight. When I was a little girl he used to bend over me after I got out of the bath and let his long, silky hair tickle my naked belly. His hair would get messy with talcum powder and baby oil. It made him smell good.

(*A period bell rings. Tutor One comes. Tutor Two and Policeman come. They all moan in unison*)

STUDENT TWO: What's that? Is my time up?

TUTOR ONE AND TUTOR TWO (*mumbling in unison*): That's all we can do for you today.

STUDENT TWO: But I still don't understand. I need more time!

(*Policeman puts on jacket with badge, crosses stage and enters Tutor Two's cubicle*)

POLICEMAN: Sorry miss, the Learning Center is closed.

(*Black Out.*)

INTERVIEW WITH LISA BURDIGE, *author of* The Tutors

Given the minimal financial rewards for writing for the stage, why do you do it?
I don't really care about the money. A long time ago I made a decision to separate my finances from my art. I write because I have something to say and I want to say it in a certain way.

Tell us something about your introduction to theater.
The first play I remember seeing was *Pippin* when I was five. I've never quite forgotten that.

What first prompted you to write plays?
I wrote whatever I wanted to and sometimes it would come out like a play. Sometimes for me, certain stories seem to be told better in certain forms.

What do you think about the state of theater in the U.S. today?
Theater in the U.S. is in a scary place. There are two camps: the highly commercial, which is just run on American capitalism and has nothing to do with art, and the struggling avant-garde, which sometimes doesn't have a lot of interest in its audience. It is more interested in just being performative.

Where do you situate theater in mainstream American culture?
On the edge, but feeding a lot of the more mainstream mediums. I don't think many people in America really pay attention to theater. It's a small community. But the people who make films (which do have a very wide audience) are influenced by theatrical works.

What were you aiming to do with *The Tutors*?
I wanted to be funny, and I was trying to present the pathos of a kind of life that I was living at the time. I was interested in juxtaposing moments to create a narrative.

NO EVIL   *by Emily Jenkins*

Characters:

Elsie—Age 13. Sees no evil, or tries not to. Seeks beauty as reassurance, condemns ugliness for the threats it offers.

Lacie—Age 13. Hears no evil, or tries not to. Criticism and unpleasant ideas disturb her greatly. Longs to hear good news.

Tillie—Age 13. Speaks no evil, or tries not to. A peacemaker. Afraid to voice unpopular or unwanted opinions.

Setting: The bottom of a well, not far from a candy store

Time: Saturday

(*Elsie, Lacie, and Tillie sit together. They each have a paper bag full of candy. Elsie has a fashion magazine, maybe two. The lights are dim.*)

ALL: Once upon a time, there were three little girls and they lived at the bottom of a well.

LACIE: What did they live on?

TILLIE AND ELSIE: They lived on treacle.

LACIE: They couldn't have done that. They'd have been ill.

TILLIE AND ELSIE: They did. And they were.

LACIE: Why did they live at the bottom of a well?

TILLIE AND ELSIE: It was a treacle well.

(*Lights up. The girls begin to rustle through their bags of candy. Their dia-*

logue should be fast and their speeches should interrupt and overlap each other. They laugh pretty often)

LACIE: Elsie, did you get redvines? I meant to get redvines and I totally forgot.

ELSIE: Yeah, yeah. But I don't think I want any of your stuff. You got all those grossy gross peanut butter jelly beans.

LACIE: What's wrong with that?

ELSIE: There's something gross about them. They remind me of little miniature shits.

TILLIE: Don't swear.

ELSIE: Oooh, big deal. Shit shit shit shit. That's what the peanut butter jelly beans are like. Little round rabbit turdies.

TILLIE: They are not. They're good. You don't like them?

ELSIE: Rabbit turdies—

LACIE: Don't say that about my candy. You'll ruin it.

ELSIE: —rabbit turdies. You don't like them either, Till. You never buy them.

ELSIE: Well, I just like green apple better. But— *(to Lacie)* I don't think they're gross at all. And they're not like rabbit turdies. They're really cute, actually.

LACIE: Thank you *very* much! So there. My candy is perfectly good. You're nice little candies, aren't you? I'm going to organize you. *(Lacie begins organizing her candy)* Elsie, can I have two redvines for three sourpusses?

ELSIE: Okay. *(Hands over two redvines)*

LACIE: Here here. *(Offers three sourpusses)*

ELSIE: No, I gotta pick them. I only like the ones where you can see the smiley face.

LACIE: Okay.

(They make the transaction and begin to eat. A moment of silence. Elsie opens a magazine)

ELSIE *(referring to a picture in the magazine)*: Lace, your boobies are practically that big, now.

LACIE *(uncertain if this is good or bad)*: Are they?

ELSIE: Aren't they, Till?

TILLIE: Yeah. You are totally bodacious, Lace.

ELSIE: Oh, yeah. They're humungoid. Todd Abrahms is always checking them out in social studies.

LACIE: Are they, really?

TILLIE: It's good, Lace. It's good to have big boobies.

LACIE: Is he, really?

TILLIE: You have to get the right bra, though.

ELSIE: Yeah, it's definitely good. The bigger the better. *(Flips through the magazine)* See, those are good ones. Those are good ones. Those are good ones. You have magazine boobs, Lacie.

TILLIE: I read somewhere that if you get big boobies you have to sleep in your bra. Do you sleep in your bra, Lace?

LACIE: Is Todd Abrahms cute?

ELSIE: Righteously cute. He's beautiful, you're beautiful, you make a beautiful couple. *(Laughs)*

TILLIE: Lace, Lace, do you sleep in your bra, I said?

LACIE: He only wrote me that one note. We're not a couple.

TILLIE: I don't know about Todd Abrahms.

LACIE: You don't know?

TILLIE: Never mind.

LACIE: You don't think he's gross do you? Oh my god.

TILLIE: No, I didn't say that, it's just—

LACIE: Oh, don't tell me, I don't want to hear it—

ELSIE: I need something different. I got too much chocolate.

LACIE: Okay, yes I do. What do you think?

ELSIE: I think he's cute. Give me another sourpuss.

LACIE: I don't have anymore.

TILLIE: I got sour lemons, you want one of those?

ELSIE: Yeah yeah, I'll give you a kiss?

TILLIE: Okay. I didn't see they had kisses.

ELSIE: They're over in the corner bin, mixed up with caramels.

TILLIE: I never saw them.

ELSIE: He's completely cute, Lacie.

LACIE: But Till—

TILLIE: I wish I got cinnamon bears.

LACIE: —was saying maybe not. If she says maybe not, maybe I say maybe not.

TILLIE: I didn't say maybe not, I said I didn't know.

LACIE: I shouldn't hear these things. They disturb my "peace of mind." That's what Rachel always says about the news. It disturbs her "peace of mind."

ELSIE: Your stepmom sounds like a freak of nature.

LACIE: And then I don't know what I think.

TILLIE: I didn't say anything at all, Lace. Just mellow.

(*A pause. They eat candy*)

ELSIE (*reading from magazine*): Here's a quiz. You ready?

TILLIE: Yup.

LACIE: Yup. No, no, wait. I want to make a trade. Till, what will you take for a watermelon? I need a watermelon.

TILLIE: Umm, what are those?

ELSIE (*reading*): Learn Your Sexual IQ. Multiple choice.

LACIE: Apple-icious.

TILLIE: Are they good?

LACIE: Uh-huh.

ELSIE: Green M&Ms make your boobs grow. True or false?

TILLIE (*to Lacie*): She made that up, right?

LACIE: Completely.

TILLIE: False false false. But I better eat one just in case. (*Eats one*)

LACIE: They're good. Give me a watermelon.

TILLIE: Okay. (*They exchange candy*)

LACIE (*to Elsie*): Do the real one.

ELSIE: Okay, okay, okay. Here it really is. Ready? Your boyfriend—

TILLIE: Todd!

LACIE: Don't say that!

ELSIE: Your boyfriend calls on Friday night at six PM to say he can't make your dinner date that evening. He doesn't offer an excuse. What do you do?

TILLIE: Is he mad at me?

ELSIE: You can't ask questions. It's multiple choice. Here we are: A. Ask him what he's doing instead. B. Hang up on him and never see him again. C. Give him a piece of your mind. D. Find out if he wants to reschedule.

LACIE: Give him my what?

TILLIE: Your peace of mind.

LACIE: Really?

ELSIE: No no, a piece of your mind. It means tell him off, tell him what you think.

LACIE: But wait, what do we think?

TILLIE: Seriously, it means we think something mean, right?

LACIE: We're mad, right?

TILLIE: No, I don't think we're mad exactly.

LACIE: We are, too. We're mad, right?

ELSIE: Yeah, I think so. Is that your answer?

(*A pause*)

LACIE: What are the other choices?

TILLIE: Ask a different one.

ELSIE: Do you want to hang up on him?

TILLIE: No, no. Ask a different one.

ELSIE: Find out if he wants to reschedule?

TILLIE: I don't know. Ask the next one.

LACIE: I'm not sure about this quiz.

ELSIE: It's not very sexy.

TILLIE: Can I see what the next part is?

(*Tillie leans over to get the magazine from Elsie, but Elsie keeps it out of her reach. Lacie's candy gets disorganized*)

LACIE: You guys! My candy!

TILLIE: Elsie! Let me see it.

ELSIE: No, no. It's mine. It'll cost you—

TILLIE: Come on.

ELSIE: —forty thousand pieces of candy.

(*Tillie and Elsie move from girlish teasing to aggressive play-fighting—like boys. It is a different quality of movement than we have seen them do before, although they continue to laugh. They punch each other on the arms, do pretend kick-boxing, and make feints toward more serious attacks.*

Lacie becomes involved in protecting her candy and putting it back in piles, studiously ignoring the unpleasantness. Tillie lands a hard one on Elsie's shoulder and the new mood dissipates)

ELSIE: Ow ow ow ow. Stop. Stop.

(*Tillie stops*)

TILLIE: Oh, sorry.

ELSIE: That totally hurt!

TILLIE: Sorry. Sorry. Are you okay?

ELSIE: No, I'm not okay. You completely hit me.

TILLIE: I didn't mean to.

LACIE: I'm sure she didn't mean to.

TILLIE: I'm sorry. Are you okay, now?

ELSIE: Yeah. I hope I'm not getting a bruise.

(*Elsie pulls up her sleeve to check*)

LACIE: It looks allright.

TILLIE: It's fine.

LACIE: It's not purple, or anything.

ELSIE: For sure?

LACIE: For sure. I would tell you if it was.

ELSIE: I really don't want to have a bruise.

LACIE: You're not going to. You're really not.

TILLIE: I'm so sorry.

(*Elsie offers Tillie and Lacie each a redvine. A pause*)

ELSIE: Now I've decided I do want a bruise. Know why?

LACIE: No. Why would you want a bruise?

ELSIE: It could be like a trend. We could all make bruises on our shoulders
with designs in them, like tattoos.

LACIE: How would you make designs?

ELSIE: With the eraser end of a pencil or something. You could press it into your arm and—

LACIE: Or you could use your fingernails.

ELSIE: —and make a flower, or your initials, or whatever you want.

TILLIE: I don't know about that.

ELSIE: It wouldn't last. It would only be there for like a week. We could all do matching ones.

TILLIE: I don't know.

LACIE: Elsie, that's really gross. Just stop talking about it right now.

TILLIE: Let's talk about the bra. I still want to know about the bra.

ELSIE: What about it?

TILLIE: Does Lacie sleep with a bra on because of her boobs?

LACIE: God, you make it sound like a disease or something.

ELSIE: No no, we told you it's a good thing.

TILLIE: Do you wear an underwire or just a regular?

ELSIE: Oh, Lace, don't ever wear the underwires. I read they cut off the circulation to your boobs and make them atrophy.

LACIE: I don't even want to know what that means.

ELSIE: It means they turn black and fall off.

TILLIE: No, no. It means they get all skinny and can't do their job properly. My uncle's arm got atrophied after he had it in a cast.

ELSIE: That's gotta be wrong. How could boobies get skinny and not do their job properly?

TILLIE: They could.

LACIE: You guys! Please stop. I'm not wearing any underwire anyway!

ELSIE: They could not. They don't have any muscles in them.

TILLIE (*sarcastic*): Oh, and they're going to turn black and fall off?

ELSIE: Well, it could happen. Lace, I really don't think you should wear the underwires.

LACIE: I already told you I don't have any of those!

(*A pause. They look at Lacie. She is clearly distraught*)

ELSIE: And if you do, don't wear it overnight, 'cause the pressure against the mattress could do something very bad to you.

TILLIE: Elsie, she's not wearing it. Right, Lace?

LACIE: I told you already.

ELSIE: Okay. I just wanted to be sure you didn't spoil your lovely boobies. (*Laughs*)

TILLIE: Todd would be disappointed.

LACIE: Stop it! He only wrote me that one note.

ELSIE: Okay. We're sorry.

TILLIE: Yes, we're sorry. We'll be good.

(*A pause*)

ELSIE: It's so obvious he likes you, Lace.

LACIE: Don't say that!

ELSIE: Why not? It's good.

TILLIE: It is, Lace.

LACIE: I thought you said you didn't know about him.

TILLIE: I didn't say anything.

LACIE: Oh.

TILLIE: Really, I didn't.

LACIE: Okay.

(*A pause*)

TILLIE: Want some chocolate?

LACIE: Yeah.

ELSIE: Me, too.

(*They eat*)

TILLIE: Everything okay?

LACIE: Yes.

TILLIE: Do you have peace of mind, now?

LACIE: Okay.

TILLIE (*to Elsie*): Do you have peace of mind now??

ELSIE: Okay.

TILLIE: Allright, then. Once upon a time there were three little girls and they lived at the bottom of a well.

ELSIE AND LACIE: What did they live on?

TILLIE: They lived on treacle.

ELSIE AND LACIE: They couldn't have done that. They'd have been ill.

TILLIE: They did. And they were.

ELSIE AND LACIE: Why did they live at the bottom of a well?

TILLIE: It was a treacle well.

INTERVIEW WITH EMILY JENKINS, author of No Evil

Tell us something about your introduction to theater.

I grew up in the theater. My father is the playwright Len Jenkins. As a kid, I used to sit in the back during rehearsals. Then I had a short-lived career as a stage actress during my adolescent years. I worked in theaters in Seattle, playing kid parts.

What first prompted you to write plays?

As a child, my first play was written to avoid having to act a major part in the show my "advanced spelling group" was going to put on. The play I wrote culminated in all the characters being sucked down a giant toilet, and we performed it in front of the whole school. As an adult, though, I began writing *No Evil* as a way of procrastinating work on my dissertation. It was composed almost entirely in the rare book room at Columbia University, where I was supposed to be researching early twentieth-century editions of *Alice's Adventures in Wonderland*. The opening lines of the play are a variation on the dormouse's story from the mad tea party.

Dramatically, what were you aiming to do with *No Evil*?

I wanted to convey the particular rhythms of speech I remembered from childhood, and I wanted to re-imagine the dormouse's tale to tell more of the story. I felt there was more to that scenario of the three little girls at the bottom of the well. I also set myself a formal challenge. Each girl is warding off evil in a particular way: one refuses to see it, one refuses to hear it, and one refuses to speak it.

What are the biggest inspirations for your writing?

I'm inspired by Jane Austen, Charles Dickens, P.G. Wodehouse, James Thurber, David Sedaris, and David Foster Wallace—for the effervescence of their language, and the way the brilliant humor never prevents them from telling stories in an urgent and compelling way.

Is there any advice you would give to aspiring playwrights?

I never had a mentor. I never had a writing teacher tell me I had any particular talent. I was never anyone's favorite student. In fact, I came out of creative writing class in college feeling totally invisible and completely intimidated. Now, I make my living writing. So I would say, go to school for writing if you must—but do it to learn the craft of storytelling, not to prove to yourself that you have talent or to see how you stack up against other people. Ignore anything anyone tells you that's in any way discouraging. Don't listen to them. Listen to the voices in your head and put them down on paper.

THE METROPOLITAN *by Mark Green*

Nighttime. A park in the Bronx. Ty and Raheim sit on a park bench. Raheim has a bandage on his cheek. They have two forty-ounce beers wrapped in brown paper bags.

TY: You down?

RAHEIM: Yeah, I'm down.

TY: You sure?

RAHEIM: Yeah, I'm sure.

TY: Allright now. He walks through here all the time.

RAHEIM: Ai'ight.

TY: We got to take care of business.

RAHEIM: I know.

TY: Can't let a nigga cut you and get away with it.

(*Ty pulls out a gun*)

RAHEIM (*referring to gun*): Keep it low.

TY: Man, chill out. No one can see. (*Ty hands the gun to Raheim*)

RAHEIM: Good to see you.

TY: Huh?

RAHEIM: Good to see you . . . away from crazy niggas . . .

TY: You know what your problem is?

RAHEIM: My problem, huh.

TY: Your problem is . . .

RAHEIM: . . . my problem is . . .

TY: Your problem is you think too much.

RAHEIM: I think too much.

TY: Think too much, yo. You let shit get to you.

RAHEIM: I know I do man, but I just wondered . . .

TY: You can't let shit bother you, yo.

RAHEIM: I know, true, but . . .

TY: You gotta do what you gotta do.

RAHEIM: Gotta do, yeah, yeah, yeah.

TY: 'Cause when shit bothers me, I get fucked up.

RAHEIM: Yeah.

TY: Drink a forty . . . hit a blunt.

RAHEIM: Right.

TY: Or both.

RAHEIM: I hear you yo, I hear you, but . . .

TY: Like that time I shot that Rican muf'fucka.

RAHEIM: Last Fourth of July.

TY: Blowing off them cherry bombs.

RAHEIM: Bad muf'fuckin' cherry bombs.

TY: We're blowing them off. These kids get too close.

RAHEIM: Yup.

TY: So I'm trying to be nice, you remember that.

RAHEIM: I remember.

TY: Can't be nice these days—and I'm like "yo kids, move y'all little asses the fuck back. Shit's dangerous." So one of them little muf'fuckas start cryin'.

RAHEIM: Right.

TY: Cryin' to his father. So Pop comes out with a gun, talking that boola, boola, bullshit, I'm like, "yo, gun!" He starts firing—"Blah! Blah! Blah! . . . we run . . .

RAHEIM: I busted my head against that Benz runnin', remember?

TY: Fly Benz, yo. That muf'fucka was fly as shit. So I'm like, "am I shot, am I shot?"

RAHEIM: And I get lightheaded, fell . . . "oh shit, I got shot!"

TY: Right.

RAHEIM: I got shot in the head! Shit was wild.

TY: Shit was wacked, yo. All that blood.

RAHEIM: And if you weren't there, yo, my ass woulda been dead.

TY: Yeah, yeah.

RAHEIM: I woulda died.

TY: Well, you know.

RAHEIM: If you didn't suck that blood out my mouth, I woulda drowned.

TY: Nasty tastin' blood too.

RAHEIM: Woulda drowned in my own blood.

TY: That's why when I went back to blow that muf'fuckin' Rican's head off, I couldn't be soft, right? Think about his kids.

RAHEIM: Right.

TY: His wife, his boys . . .

RAHEIM: I hear that.

TY: All I could to do was think of you. Didn't want nobody fuckin' with my boy, right—you in the hospital . . . tubes all up your nose.

RAHEIM: Kept talking to myself—"You got a bullet in your skull . . . chill out . . . you can make it, you can . . ."

TY: He fucked with you, he fucked with me.

RAHEIM: . . . shit was rough man, no lie . . .

TY: And I ain't to be fucked with. You know what I'm sayin'? Don't fuck with me!

RAHEIM: Right.

TY: I'm the wrong muf'fucka to fuck with.

RAHEIM: You right about that.

TY: You just can't worry about shit. You shoot the nigga. We move on.

(*Pause*)

RAHEIM: So when we gonna hook up again?

TY: Hook up? What we doing now?

RAHEIM: Not like this . . . I mean, away . . .

TY: I don't understand you, yo.

RAHEIM: What you mean?

TY: You get a bullet in your head, you get soft on me.

RAHEIM: It ain't like that.

TY: All you want to do is be alone, staring out into the stars and shit.

RAHEIM: Well, you know . . .

TY: It's like you afraid of icing that muf'fucka for cuttin' you.

RAHEIM: I got a lot on my mind.

TY: Man, in the old days, you, Mad Dog Raheim wouldn't have nothing on your mind. You, Mad Dog Raheim, wouldn't let no bitch ass nigga cut him like that. You, Mad Dog Raheim, would have gone off.

RAHEIM: Ain't mad no more. Ain't a dog no more.

TY: Mad Dog Raheim woulda iced the nigga who cut him. Now I got to hold your hand like a muf'fuckin' bitch just to off this muf'fucka.

RAHEIM: It ain't worth it.

TY: Ain't worth it? Look, you gotta do what you gotta do. Gotta let that nigga know you ain't weak. And that we, your boys, ain't weak.

RAHEIM: I know, I know, but . . .

TY: If you don't ice that nigga for cuttin' you, he's gonna think you're weak. If he thinks you're weak, he's gonna think we're weak. And that muf'fucka can't think we're weak. (*Beat*) So you may not want to ice him, but it ain't just about you, know what I'm saying. It's about all of us. Your boys around the way, not just you Raheim. Kill him for us, if not for your-self. (*Beat*) Just stop thinking so damn much. (*Pause*)

RAHEIM: I hate the Bronx!

TY: What?

RAHEIM: I hate all the Bronx, I want out!

TY: Where you gonna go man? That's what I want to know. Where you gonna go?

(*Pause*)

RAHEIM: I got something to say.

TY: What, muf'fucka? What you got to say?

(*Raheim grabs Ty and kisses him on the lips*)

TY: Man, what's up like that?!

RAHEIM: It's all good.

TY: What muf'fucka?! Oh shit . . . someone coulda . . .

RAHEIM: When we gonna hook up again?

TY: You're tripping, man. We're down like that only in private, yo. Only in private . . . oh shit, someone coulda seen . . . (*Raheim begins to laugh*) You laughing? You trying to get us killed?

RAHEIM: . . . oh man . . . you know . . . I never told you. I never told anyone . . . but I like to read magazines now.

TY: So, motha fucka?

(*Raheim pulls a magazine from his socks*)

RAHEIM: *Metropolitan Homes*, man.

TY: Yo, yo, keep that low, okay.

RAHEIM: *Metropolitan Homes*, man. And I open those pages and I walk into the magazine man. Walk right into it and out of the Bronx.

TY: You are trying to get us killed.

RAHEIM: I want a big house, man. Outside the city. With trees all around. And a lake.

(*Ty looks into the distance*)

TY: Is that the muf'fucka who sliced you?

RAHEIM: And in our master bedroom . . .

TY: Our master bedroom?

RAHEIM: . . . our furniture will be arranged in magical places from which we can contemplate the views of the lawn, woods and the lake beyond. The colors of our room will be in neutral tones . . . raffia wall coverings.

TY: What muf'fucka?

RAHEIM: Neutral-colored raffia wall covering. So with the morning sunlight, this room will be charming and elegant. This simple open-air structure will consist of white-washed beams, marble columns, and the ubiquitous terra cotta tile roof.

TY (*looking into the distance*): Get your gun. That looks like him coming.

RAHEIM: There'll be two small tables around our beds, two oval-shaped tables with several concentric borders with leaf patterns.

TY: Take out your gun.

RAHEIM: There'll be two chairs, each one imbued with the wit and vitality that are the essence of good design.

TY: Your gun, nigga, pull out your gun.

RAHEIM: Over here, we'll have an empire gondola chair of pine with a faux-mahogany finish.

TY: Man, why you trippin'?

RAHEIM: And finally our bed: a king-sized bed with floral bed coverings in pink with canopies of peach and apricot.

TY: Are you gonna shoot the motha fucka or what?

RAHEIM: With a collection of antique needlework of animal pictures. This will be an elegant country room without a clichéd country look. Romantic yet disciplined.

(*Ty takes the gun from Raheim*)

TY: Give me the muf'fuckin' gun, he's turning around.

RAHEIM: Then outside the window, I'll plant olive trees, cypress, myrtle, and holly oak. Some broom and bray. And then I'll get in the covers and take you with me, and I'll never get out. And I'll never have to see the Bronx again. And it will be you and me. Just you and me.

(*Ty shoots Raheim in the head. Stillness. Ty pops open a beer and drinks it down quickly. Fade to black.*)

INTERVIEW WITH MARK GREEN, author of The Metropolitan

Tell us something about your introduction to theater.

My parents took me to see *The Wiz* when I was about twelve years old. I had no idea theater could be so exciting. And what put the nail in the coffin for me was that I saw *A Streetcar Named Desire* on TV. I was riveted. It blew me away. From then on I wanted to be a writer.

What first prompted you to write plays?

When I went to France for summer school I got really depressed, and I started writing about my depression. That became my first play. I sent it to a theater called the Rainbow Repertory Theater, a black gay company. And they did it!

What is your professional background as a playwright?

The experience with Rainbow Rep was crucial. We took the play to Harlem. It was the first time the National Black Theater presented a black gay play—and it was really exciting to provoke the audience, a black audience used to traditional structures and content. Theater is so dead for the most part. I want to rock the boat—not in a hostile way, but counterbalancing aggression with healing, revelation, epiphany.

How would you characterize your writing?

There are a lot of political issues I'm concerned with. As a writer I try to personalize everything to avoid didacticism. I use some traditional structures, but then I play around with the sense of place and time that I've established. I'm borrowing from classical traditions, then disrupting them.

What were you aiming to do with *The Metropolitan*?

I went to an all black college in D.C., and when I went to the Dramatic Writing Program at NYU it was the first time I went to school with a lot of white people. I found I had to move through people's notions of blackness— stereotypes—in order to connect with the other students and with the faculty. With *The Metropolitan*, I wanted to take elements of the homeboy type and invert them, so we can experience the inner life of one of those characters. I did a shift in language that wasn't a naturalistic shift, but which reflected his inner life. I like being ahead of the audience, surprising them with horror and unexpected beauty.

Who are the biggest influences for your writing?

Suzan-Lori Parks, for her pure audacity to run with an impulse in a way that is really about her. Especially in her early work, she seems to have little concern if we understand her plays. She gave me room to expand outside my comfort zone.

Art that breaks away from classical forms really turns me on, and can help inform my writing. For example, Cezanne can evoke so much with just a limited color palette, and I might restrict and discipline my language the same way.

Is there any advice you would give to aspiring playwrights?

Break the rules, but know the rules that you're breaking. Offend the audience if you need to, but do it from a high place. Provoke us and know that we can be better people in the end.

CYCLONE OF RAGE   by David Lindsay-Abaire

Characters:

Barb—A generally angry woman in her thirties.

Doctor—A generally friendly and accommodating man in his forties.

Setting: The play takes place in a doctor's office.

A psychiatrist's office. Barb, a generally angry woman, sits waiting. The generally friendly and accommodating Doctor enters.

DOCTOR: Hello, I'm Dr. Carlson. I'm sorry to keep you waiting. There was a crowd outside. A man threw himself in front of a hansom cab. I wanted to make sure it wasn't one of my patients. I love the expression hansom cab because it sounds like handsome cab. (*Chuckles*) You must be Barbara Figgits. Why don't you sit down?

BARB: Why don't you kiss my fat Irish ass?

DOCTOR (*smiles*): Allright, you can stand if you'd like. Do you mind if I sit? Suicides always make me a little woozy.

BARB: I don't care if you do a Russian split and rip your asshole open.

DOCTOR: Thank you, then I'll sit. It turns out it wasn't a patient at all. Just Gary up in Accounts Payable, covered with hoofprints. They had to shoot the horse. Quite a show. You're not suicidal, I hope.

BARB: No I'm not, you mutant cock-faced son-of-a-bitchin', prick-wad.

DOCTOR: Oh good. I understand Mr. Rottlesberg asked you come see me.

BARB: That freakin' bastard.

DOCTOR: You think your fiancé is a freakin' bastard?

BARB: That walking sausage fart is not my fiancé.

DOCTOR: He's not?

BARB: No.

DOCTOR: You don't refer to him as your fiancé?

BARB: No.

DOCTOR: I see. What do you call him?

BARB: I call him Dick-Cheese. Sometimes I call him Ass-Wipe or Stupid Fat-Head Motherfucker.

DOCTOR: Uh-huh. But not fiancé?

BARB: Are you deaf, you muddle-headed cocksucking retard?

DOCTOR: No, I'm not deaf.

BARB: That needle-dick lard-ass is not my fiancé. Next question!

DOCTOR: Very well. Mr. Rottlesberg seems to think that—

BARB (*interrupting*): Oh, he thinks?! Has Jesus performed another fuckin' miracle? Well walk on water and gimme a million fishes cause Frank Numb-Nuts had a thought!

DOCTOR: Do you enjoy swearing?

BARB: Does the Pope shit in the woods?

DOCTOR: I don't know. (*Offers her candy*) Licorice?

BARB: No thank you.

DOCTOR: I love licorice! (*Eats some*) Now then, as I was saying, Mr. Rottlesberg seems to think that you have a problem with anger.

BARB: Does he?

DOCTOR: He says you're a cyclone of rage.

BARB: And?

DOCTOR: And what?

BARB (*challenging him*): Do you agree with him?

DOCTOR: Uh . . . well . . . it's a little hard to say for sure at this juncture.

BARB: I hate you. I want to bite your head. If Frank didn't give me that giant bag of money, I wouldn't be here!

DOCTOR: Mr. Rottlesberg bribed you to come here?

BARB (*pulls a hypodermic needle from her bag*): Your face makes me nauseated. I want to puke on you.

DOCTOR (*referring to needle*): What is that?

BARB: It's a hypodermic needle (*Stabs him with it*)

DOCTOR: Ow! You stabbed me!

BARB: Yes. When people make me mad, I stab them with this needle.

DOCTOR: You can't just stab people.

BARB: Yes I can. (*Stabs him again*)

DOCTOR: Ow! Quit it!

BARB: There's nothing in it. It's just a needle.

DOCTOR: But it hurts!

BARB: It's sterile, you whining sack of piss.

DOCTOR: I think you should leave. (*He is stabbed again*) Ow! Get out of my office.

BARB: No, I'm starting to like it here. (*Stabs him again*)

DOCTOR: Ms. Figgits, stop stabbing me!

BARB: Oh, allright! (*Puts needle away*) I can never have any fun.

DOCTOR: You obviously have a problem. Now that you've stopped puncturing me, can we talk about your rage?

BARB: What rage? (*Applying band-aids to his wounds*) Mr. Rottlesberg seems to think you have some problems with your father, but you don't like to talk about them.

BARB: Are you a faggot?

DOCTOR: I beg your pardon?

BARB: A queer, a homo, a limp-wristed fudge packer. Are you a tutti-frutti? I don't care if you are. I don't judge people.

DOCTOR: We're not here to discuss me, Ms. Figgits.

BARB: Aren't we, doctor? Aren't we here to discuss whatever I want to talk about?

DOCTOR: Tell me about your father.

BARB: Tell me about your boyfriend.

DOCTOR: No.

BARB: Faggot-ass.

DOCTOR (*rings a bell*): No name-calling in my office! You lose three points! (*Makes note of that*)

BARB (*momentarily confused*): I do? Three points?

DOCTOR: Yes. Now you'll have to work very hard to earn them back. (*Pulls out a file*)

BARB: Allright.

DOCTOR (*perusing file*): I understand your father left the family when you were quite young.

BARB: How do I earn points back?

DOCTOR: I guess you'll have to figure that out now, won't you? As I was saying, your father abandoned you and started hanging around the train yards, playing poker with the local hobos. And one day he snuck onto a departing cattle car and rode off. He soon became known as Box Car Charlie, and he's been riding the rails ever since. You haven't heard from him in years. Is all this true?

BARB: No. That's the plot of a Mickey Rooney movie called Box Car Charlie. I told Frank that's what happened and he believed me. Frank is very stupid.

DOCTOR: Yes, I'm starting to see that. Now, why don't you tell me what really happened with your father.

BARB: My legs are tired. Can I sit now?

DOCTOR: If you want to.

BARB: In your chair?

DOCTOR: No. I'm sitting in my chair. You can sit in the patient's chair.

BARB (*pulls out needle again*): I want to sit in your chair! Move it, you shit-spewing colostomy bag!

DOCTOR (*runs away from his chair*): Don't prick me!

BARB (*sits in chair*): Oh yes, this is much better. Very comfortable. Can I have some licorice now?

DOCTOR: Do you promise to behave?

BARB: I'll try.

DOCTOR: Crow like a rooster.

BARB: What?

DOCTOR: I was raised on a farm, and the sounds of barnyard animals soothe me. So if you would like to earn one point back, and also get a piece of licorice, then you must crow like a rooster.

BARB: So that's your game, is it? Very well. (*She crows like a rooster. He rings his bell*)

DOCTOR: A plus! For that you get one point and one piece of licorice. (*Gives her licorice*)

BARB (*chewing*): Thank you, doctor.

DOCTOR: Tell me, Ms. Figgits, do you think your relationship with your father has anything to do with your irrational outbursts?

BARB (*eating licorice, bouncing in chair*): I don't know what you're talking about. This chair is very bouncy. You should try it. Sit on my lap.

DOCTOR: I don't want to.

BARB: Sit on my lap!

(*Doctor runs to her and sits on her lap. They both bounce in the chair*)

BARB: Wahoo! This is fun, isn't it?! Ride 'em cowboy.

DOCTOR: It reminds me of my days on the open plain.

BARB: Atta boy! Giddyap!

DOCTOR: Yippy kiyay!

BARB (*stops suddenly*): Okay, you're too heavy. Move! (*Shoves him off her lap onto the floor*) You were putting my legs to sleep.

DOCTOR: Ow, my knees. You've hurt me.

BARB: Tough-titty.

DOCTOR: You play too rough. I don't think this is going to work out.

BARB: You give up so easily.

DOCTOR: Ms. Figgits—

BARB: You can call me Barb.

DOCTOR: Ms. Figgits, I've been your fiancé's doctor for several years—

BARB: He's not my fiancé.

DOCTOR: And we have spent many sessions talking about you and the way you treat that poor man. I've always thought he exaggerated matters, and as a favor to him I agreed to meet with you to get to the bottom of things. Now I've come to learn that he was not, in fact, exaggerating. You're evidently insane and I feel compelled to tell Mr. Rottlesberg to leave you.

BARB: No, please. I'll tell you everything.

DOCTOR: I'm afraid it's too late for that.

BARB: My father raised chinchillas in our basement, and sold their furs to the black market.

DOCTOR: I've heard enough, Ms. Figgits.

BARB: When I misbehaved, he would lock me in an old steamer trunk with seven or eight of the rodents, and throw the trunk down the basement stairs. The commotion disoriented the chinchillas, inciting them to sink their teeth into my little legs as we tumbled in the darkness. I still have scars. And I never forgave my father for his brutality.

DOCTOR (*having been suckered in by the story*)**:** Mother of god, is all that true?

BARB: No, it's the plot of a Fred McMurray film called *A Trunk Load of Chinchillas.*

DOCTOR: There's no such movie! You're just full of lies. All lies. Just like my Pa! That back-stabbing old cow-poke! Damn him and his beef jerky!

BARB: I thought this was about me?!

DOCTOR: Get out of my office!

BARB: One more chance! Only the truth now! I promise!

DOCTOR: I'm sorry, I can't.

(Barbara moos seductively. This pleases the doctor)

DOCTOR: Goddamn you woman, you play me like a banjo. That's one more point, but you're still in the hole.

BARB: Oh doctor, that's very naughty of you to say.

DOCTOR: It is? I don't think so. The truth now!

BARB: My mother was an unhappy woman. She slept with several hot dog vendors up and down Central Park West. My father got wind of her trysts and was enraged. My mother and I were crossing West 58th Street when my father appeared out of nowhere and killed her. Ever since then, I've had problems with men. I'm afraid that if I marry that festering scab Frank, he'll turn on me and do what my father did to my mother.

DOCTOR: Which was?

BARB: He ran her down. Ran her over . . . with a hansom cab.

DOCTOR: I love that expression.

BARB: He used to give rides through Central Park. But now he's in prison. And I am left with this bubbling anger. Whenever I see a hansom cab now, I have to throw someone in front of it. Can you help me, doctor?

DOCTOR (*he considers the case*): Perhaps. It'll take hundreds of sessions and thousands of dollars, but I think perhaps I can.

BARB: Oh, thank you doctor.

DOCTOR (*rings his bell*): Another point. There, we're even today.

BARB: Can I have another piece of licorice?

DOCTOR: Only if you come back again next week at this time.

BARB: Of course.

DOCTOR: And gobble like a turkey.

(*She gobbles. He rings his bell*)

DOCTOR: For a good gobble you get one piece of licorice. (*Gives her licorice*)

BARB: Goodbye, doctor.

DOCTOR: Say hello to Frank.

BARB: I would, but I smothered him in his sleep last night.

DOCTOR (*chuckles*): Allright then. See you next week.

BARB: Ta-ta!

(*She exits. Blackout.*)

INTERVIEW WITH DAVID LINDSAY-ABAIRE, author of Cyclone of Rage

What is your background as a playwright?

I studied acting at Sarah Lawrence and took playwriting on the side, mostly to fill up my program. It was either playwriting or "mask work" and I wasn't a big mask fan at the time (I've since grown to really appreciate masks and often wonder whether I made the right decision). Anyway, it seemed I couldn't shake the playwriting bug. I continued with it through Sarah Lawrence, wrote a couple of plays there, got a couple of productions, and somehow managed to get into the Julliard Playwriting program, which is run by Marsha Norman and Christopher Durang. It was there that I really started to take playwriting seriously, and I learned to accept that this whim of mine might actually pan out.

What first prompted you to write plays?

I started writing plays in high school. Our tenth grade class got together and decided to put on a show. It was very Mickey Rooney. We decided who would act in it, who would direct, where we would get lights, and then someone turned to me and said "Well, you're the funny one, you should write it." And that was that. I was a playwright. I look back on that day sometimes and think, If only that girl had turned to me and said 'Hey, you've got delicate fingers, you be a brain surgeon.' I'd be a very rich man right now.

Tell us something about your introduction to theater.

My uncle was in a production of a play about the life of Jesus Christ, and he asked if I wanted to play Jesus as a boy. I had one scene where Jesus goes to a temple and asks all sorts of obnoxious questions to the priests. I'm sure I was terrible. The production was terrible. The grown up Jesus was fifty pounds overweight. His gut hung out during the crucifixion. The actor playing Pontius Pilate was a drug addict, and Mary Magdalene stuttered. It was insane, and that was all it took. I knew I wanted a life in the theater.

What are the biggest influences/inspirations for your writing?

Ionesco, Feydau, John Guare, Tina Howe, Sam Shepard, Chekhov, Joe Orton. And then random stuff like 19th century Russian novelists, namely Tolstoy and Dostoevski. Anyone with an overdeveloped sense of irony or absurdity. You put all those writers into a pot, you mix the zaniness of Feydeau with the dark undercurrent of Dostoevski, and you come up with something close to my writing.

Given the minimal financial rewards for writing for the stage, why do you do it?

Because I'm in control. Film and television is much more of a business. In Hollywood, writers are hired to do a job, and usually that job entails making money for a studio. So of course the writers voice or vision is waaaay down the list of priorities to the people who are writing the checks. So inevitably the writing gets watered down, overly manipulated and "developed" into the ground. In theater, it's much more unadulterated. I can create a work that is wholly my own. I own it and no one can change a word. Of course theater is collaborative, but ultimately it begins and ends with the writer and not some halfwit executive in L.A.

Is there any advice you would give to aspiring playwrights?

Keep writing new things. Don't spend three years on one play. Yes rewrite, but don't dwell. I know people who work on the same play for years, thinking they're improving it little by little, and some day they're going to get it just right. It'll never happen. You start a play with an impulse. A year later, you are a totally different person, with different feelings about the world, and you look at that play and say "Oh wait, this isn't what that play is about, it's about THIS instead," and they re-attack it, thinking they're making progress. They're not. That initial impulse is gone. Now they have a new impulse, which belongs to a NEW play. Don't put your new play feelings into an old play. Write the new play! Don't keep going back to that old one. Move on. Keep writing. Keep discovering.

OEDIPUS RETCHED! *By Dennis Davis*

A crate. The front panel falls off. Inside is a small after-hours club. A tiny stage with a red and soiled crushed velvet rug.

A microphone and stand. The floor is schmeared with crushed tomatoes and spoiled lettuce heads. Inside, the Stand-Up Messenger takes the tiny stage entering through the red sateen curtains. The Stand-Up Messenger has a classic bridge and tunnel sound.

THE STAND-UP MESSENGER: So's, there's this blind cat, Tiresias. He knew the skinny, the whole kit and caboodle from top to bottom. And for him, the Gods made it plain, ya kill ya father, ya marry ya mother, one thing leads to another, ya got yaself a complex. But take a look at me, I'm getting ahead of myself!

So's, there's this married couple who goes to the neighborhood church, and one day, the priest says some jumbo like, I was talking to God today, and I have some good news and I have some bad news. And the queen wife, she's like, well what's the good news? And the priest says, our father up in the heavens says youse are gonna have a baby. And the king man is like, great, so what's the bad news? And the priest says, the baby's gonna kill you, then fuck your wife. And do I have to tell you, the king man flips the fuck out. I mean, he's like, we gotta kill the fucking baby, and the queen wife's like, oh no, we can just hide the baby, and they take it back and forth, kill the baby, hide the baby, kill the baby, hide the baby, kill the baby, hide the baby. And the man blows his fucking stack, enough all fucking ready, am I the king of my castle, or what? Am I, or am I not, the be all that fucking ends all? When I say kill the fucking baby, I mean you better kill the fucking baby, you better jump up and down on the bed, throw yourself down a fucking flight a stairs, load yourself on fifty or sixty comet shakes, and if in nine months, you still ain't killed this baby, I want you to take the fucking pecker wood, string him up like a chicken and throw him off the highest fuckin' mountain, do I make myself perfectly fucking clear, puddnin' and pie. And the queen's like, yes, baby cakes, you make yourself perfectly effin' clear. And the king's like, and do me a favor, I don't want to ever hear tell of this shit, ever the fuck again. And he didn't, so to speak.

So's, we jumps a few years and skips to another part of town, right? And we find this gimp kid, right? Who was what? Raised by fucking wild sheep on some mountaintop? Wrong. This rich couple makes like Ma and Pa Kent and take him in, right? And they call him Eddie Puss, which means like "sick foot" or "flat foot" or some such ridiculousness, which really don't matter anyway, 'cause it's just icing on the frigging cake. So's, Eddie Puss grows up and runs away from home, and he meets these tough guys crossing a bridge, and they want to throw down. And Eddie's like, I just want to cross the bridge, and the tough guys are like, no, you let us cross the bridge. So, Eddie catches this high falooting, frigging attitude, and he hits the tough guys, and the tough guys hit Eddie, and one thing leads to another and the tough guys are layed out frigging dead. And would you believe it, the head dead tough guy, Lay-Us, the name sounds pretty queer to me, dum-dadum-dum dum, turns out to be Eddie's father.

So's, there's you go, one fucking, prophetic prophecy down, two to go.

So's, more sooners than laters, Eddie meets up with this other cat, Griphon Jones, who actually is this cat thing, come sphincter monster, and oh so, so much, more. And Griphon's running this protection racket, on this one town, Thebes. So's, Eddie's like, cool, I'm no fool, not my problem, not my business, just let me pass. And Griphon's like, pass my ass, here's a riddle, what's green and smells like pork? And Eddie's like, what's green and smells like pork, what's green and smells like pork, DO I LOOK LIKE A FUCKING RETARD OR WHAT, Kermit's middle finger. And Griphon Jones blows his fucking stack. I mean it. Literally. His head blows right the fuck off his shoulders. And then these Thebans come running out, and they're like, Kermit's middle finger, Kermit's middle finger, fucking hey, boy genius, why don't you be our king? And Eddie's like, no fucking way. And the Thebans are like, way Dude, there's just one catch, ya gotta marry the queen. And Eddie's like, hey, tell me more. And the Thebans are like, well, she's this hot, old dame, named Jocasta. And Eddie's like, Jocasta? Jocasta? You cast her, I don't even know her. And they all crack the fuck up, slap up backs, and push comes to shove and Eddie marries the old dame. And don't tell me it's not a small world after all, can you guess who the fuck this chick is? You got it, his fucking mother!

So's, the drum rolls please, two effin' prophetic prophecies down, one to go.

So's everything's hunky-dory, Eddie is a cool king, Jocasta is a kicking queen. I mean, they really hit it off, and have not one, not two, not three, but four little rugrats, which is a whole, other damn story, I don't even have to get into. And then alls of a sudden, there's this biblical plague thing, locusts, droughts, whirlwinds, fucking erupting volcanoes, the whole nine hundred yards. And the Thebans are like, hey, fucking boy genius, get us out of this one! And Eddie, being the great fucking king he is gets on the case, and's like, WHAT TO DO? WHAT TO DO? SWEET MOTHER OF HOLY JESUS, WHAT THE FUCK TO DO?

So's, thens they all pray to fucking Zeus almighty, and slaughter this fucking pig. Now's we're back to the part where the shit hit the goddamn fan! The blind cat, Tireseas, turns out to be a real freaky-deak, rolls around in this bloody pig shit and sees fucking visions. Eddie finds out Lay-Us was his father, Jocasta is his mother and everything is all hell and high water. Jocasta screams bloody fucking murder and runs around like a chicken with its head cut off, then she hangs herself in her fucking Donna Karan original. Eddie groans and moans, I CAN'T BELIEVE I DID THE DO WITH MY MOTHER, I CAN'T BELIEVE I DID THE DO WITH MY MOTHER, and then finally, we get to prophetic prophecy numero tres, Eddie gets this sick-foot complex and sticks huge fucking pins in his eyes, and his sockets gush blood, and his little girls scream like fucking mimi's and cry, OUR FATHER IS OUR BROTHER, OUR FATHER IS OUR BROTHER, and they bang their little heads into the wall, and the people of Thebes join in this communal puke-fest, and the whole scene is just a bloody, fucked-up mess. I'm about to lose my lunch just talking about it.

So's, alls of a sudden, Eddie Puss's like, KILL ME ALREADY, KILL ME ALREADY, and the Thebans are like, KILL YOU? KILL YOU? WE DON'T EVEN KNOW YOU. WHO THE FUCK ARE YOU? WHY DON'T YOU TAKE A LONG WALK, OFF A SHORT FUCKING PIER. So's, that's what Eddie Puss did, but because he was blind as a motherfuck, he never could find the pier, so's he just kept walking and walking and walking, which is a whole, other damn story, I don't even have time to get into.

(A flash. A giant metal hook snags the crate and drags the Stand-Up Messenger and the small after-hours club out of sight)

INTERVIEW WITH DENNIS DAVIS, author of Oedipus Retched!

Tell us something about your introduction to theater.

At the bicentennial fair at my elementary school we had to perform vignettes of the revolutionary war. I was very diligent, memorizing both sets of lines, reciting them, call-and-response, alone in my room. My parents asked, "Denny, who's in that room with you?" I answered, "No one," and they returned with—a very nervous silence. That pretty much set the stage for the next twenty years or so.

What first prompted you to write plays?

I started as an actor and director making collaborative works: booking theater space, sketching outlines, having actors jump through improv-hoops, then writing the play from the work generated—usually on napkins and used envelopes. Paula Vogel brought me to Brown and forced me to write on the page, rather than directing fixes into my work or relying on group exercises to stimulate it.

Dramatically, what were you aiming to do with *Oedipus Retched?*

I was investigating the role of the messenger, structurally and as a contemporary figure. I was interested in writing for a single recognizable voice and compacting the tragedy, foregrounding the farce by compressing time.

What are the biggest influences on your writing?

My teachers Robbie McCauley and Paula Vogel. They've forged careers creating smart and provocative work. Robbie taught me the value of risk and content-as-form. Paula guided me to find style and structural design on the page. They contributed immensely to my understanding and acceptance of myself as an outsider—gay and working class—and the vantage point that lends me as a writer.

What is your professional life as a playwright?

My early career involved hustling and getting shows up for no money with a lot of energy and regularity. Nowadays, I've become the king of staged-readings, teaching gigs, and fellowship deadlines. I know this is par for the course, and I am lucky to have small venues in New York and the region presenting my work in some form or another.

Voices from the Urban Sprawl

One of these days, I'mma kill that bitch. God as my word. Talking about things that don't make no goddamn sense whatsoever. When I lay awake at night, I want to hear sounds of gunshots and domestic moanings. Not some shriveled-up geechee bitch with a penchant for tall tales.

—J.R. Riddick, *Icebox*

Yeah, so then she says to me that I don't know shit and that I never knew shit and she turns her back on me. Her back! On me! The fuckin' unofficial king of the western hemisphere. All right?! And then she did this other thing, a . . . a kind of thing that I don't even wanna talk about over here.

—John Poglinco, *Over Here*

Your personality was instantly Selwyn-Lumped special order by Prestigious top brass this is the news lady this is the news you're living with an alternate persona template a safety precaution to protect you from ESPER a mercenary telepath/abduction unit . . .

—Daniel Aukin, *Saucy Paper*

OVER HERE   *by John Poglinco*

For Joseph Ahearn

Characters:

One guy

Another guy

Time: During mass

Place: A Catholic church

One Guy and Another Guy stand in front of two chairs. They are dressed in tacky jogging suits and wear gold chains.

ONE GUY: Yeah, so then she says to me that I don't know shit and that I never knew shit and she turns her back on me. Her back! On me! The fuckin' unofficial king of the western hemisphere. All right?! And then she did this one thing, a . . . a kind of thing that I don't even wanna talk about over here.

ANOTHER GUY: What kind of thing could possibly happen that you don't wanna talk about over here? If not here, where? You see what I'm sayin'?

ONE GUY: Yeah I see what you're sayin', but I'd rather not even address that thing, okay?

(*They both sit*)

ONE GUY: 'Cause I don't even want to fuckin' dignify it with my time and your time because of the general limitations of time we're workin' with over here, all right?

(*They both kneel*)

ANOTHER GUY: Give me a hint.

ONE GUY: I'm not gonna even start dealing in hints over here because I'm not the answer man, okay? That's not my job over here nor is that my purpose at this point in time. And I'm not the hint man either, just in case you were getting confused, all right? Can you at least understand that much? And if I do start dropping you hints, tossing you a few spotty hints here and there, you're gonna want the whole thing. (*Beat*) And I'm not prepared in any way, shape or form to give you this thing in this kind of environment over here, all right? I'm sorry, but that's the way it is, so you better just beam up to that fact right now and save yourself and all of us some of the grief we all know you love to spread around town like it's goin' outta style.

ANOTHER GUY: What are you preparing to do, if you are in fact preparing to do something over here? (*They both stand*) Or maybe you're just jerkin' my chain, all right? That's all I wanna know, okay?

ONE GUY: Wait a minute. Wait. Hold on. What kind of a question is that, mister? I want you to clarify that right now! What do I look like over here, some kind of dirtbag that just walked in off the street with no agenda? Huh? With no clue? I'm not going to address that question, okay?

ANOTHER GUY: Okay, don't. I don't want you to put yourself out. I don't want you to exhaust yourself for nothing. I know how weary you get sometimes.

ONE GUY: Okay, I'm not gonna address that question, but I am gonna tell you this much.

ANOTHER GUY: How much?

ONE GUY: As much as is necessary.

ANOTHER GUY: And how much is that?

ONE GUY: More than a nugget.

ANOTHER GUY: How much more?

ONE GUY: Enough to get you by.

ANOTHER GUY: For how long?

ONE GUY: A little while.

ANOTHER GUY: That could add up.

ONE GUY: Maybe.

ANOTHER GUY: We'll see, won't we?

ONE GUY: We shall see.

ANOTHER GUY: Okay.

(*They both sit*)

ONE GUY: She was jiggling her ass at me, okay? Her ass! At me! All right? She was jiggling her ass at me when she was walkin' away with a contemptuous flourish like I have never ever seen, before this time that I'm talkin' about now.

ANOTHER GUY: When was this time?

ONE GUY: Now. This time. This thing I'm talkin' about over here!

ANOTHER GUY: Was this thing a gesture of some kind?

ONE GUY: What?!

ANOTHER GUY: The way she shook her ass at you?

ONE GUY: No, it was much much more than a gesture, okay? And there was much much more going on at that time that you don't even know about. How can you possibly ask such a question? I feel like you're not respecting the gravity of this thing that was beginning that I'm fuckin' tryin' to share with you over here.

ANOTHER GUY: I think you should continue to share this with me.

(*They both kneel*)

ONE GUY: Well . . . let me . . . let me draw out with what happened and maybe you can try and listen a little harder if it's not too much trouble to let this thing unfold with a little bit of dignity, if that's not asking too much of you.

ANOTHER GUY: You ask a lot.

ONE GUY: Yes, but I give so much in return.

ANOTHER GUY: We'll see how much.

ONE GUY: We will, won't we?

ANOTHER GUY: Yes.

ONE GUY: She knows how that ass of hers drives me to a state of distraction. All right? I see her behind and I become mute with lust. It was a manner of punctuating the thing that she had just told me to my face about me not knowing shit. Okay?

ANOTHER GUY: I think I'm following you now.

ONE GUY: Good. And then I overheard her later talkin' up a real storm. But she didn't know that I was like the fly on the wall listening to this thing that was being said. That's when I overheard her. You know what I'm sayin'?

ANOTHER GUY: You were privy to these things she was sayin'.

ONE GUY: And to the things the people who were listening were saying as they were listening to what she had the gall to be saying in the first place.

ANOTHER GUY: I think I see what you're sayin'.

(*Another Guy stands. One Guy remains kneeling*)

ONE GUY: No you don't, 'cause you don't know what it was that she was sayin'. The content of what was being said at that point in time.

ANOTHER GUY: So now you're gonna tell me, right?

ONE GUY: Correct me if I'm wrong or out of line, but that's what I'm fuckin' doin' over here. All right?

ANOTHER GUY: That's what you think you're doin', but what you're really doin' is killin' me over here with this long line you're drawing out over here.

ONE GUY: If you would just give me a chance, a little breathing room for a change, I could—

ANOTHER GUY: I'm tryin' to—

ONE GUY: You don't seem to be trying at all for all I can see.

ANOTHER GUY: Well I am.

ONE GUY: I'm just not picking up on that. Okay?

ANOTHER GUY: Look harder.

(*One Guy stands*)

ONE GUY: I'm gonna pretend that I didn't hear that, okay? Because I don't wanna get involved with a contradiction thing here between you and me and I don't wanna lose my temper. All I know is that I plant a tree, a small sapling, and you have a perverse need to kill it right away. I buy a small pet, maybe a bird at the pet store, and you crush it without remorse. I don't know why you do these things, but you do. So let's just leave it at that for the time being. All right?

ANOTHER GUY: Okay . . .

ONE GUY (*beat*): She didn't know that I was around and that vicious tongue of hers was unleashed, flappin' in her head besmirching my good name by way of maligning my character. So get this. She told "The Big Guy" behind my back, but not out of earshot, that I am so useless that she wouldn't even send me out for sandwiches.

ANOTHER GUY: Which big guy?

ONE GUY: Excuse me? I'm sorry. Did you say something?

ANOTHER GUY: Which big guy?

ONE GUY: "The Big Guy," okay? There's only one "Big Guy." All right? You obviously don't know what the situation is over here or you wouldn't be fuckin' hammering my hands to the cross like this. Am I making myself perfectly clear? So if you can just please pull these nails out of my crucifix for a few minutes and let me go free, I would appreciate that very much. Okay?

ANOTHER GUY: Hey, wait a minute. Wait.

ONE GUY: What? What? What the hell do you want from me over here?

ANOTHER GUY: You said there's only one "Big Guy"?

ONE GUY: That's right. Do I have to explain everything or what? If there was more than one "Big Guy" he wouldn't be "The Big Guy." Okay? That's not to say that there aren't other guys who are very, very big, but there's only one "Big Guy."

(*They both sit*)

ANOTHER GUY: How big is he?

ONE GUY: Don't start in with this again, all right? This beating of a dead horse thing you love to do all the time, okay? Because I'm going to refuse to acknowledge that question over here.

ANOTHER GUY: Just wait a minute—

ONE GUY: How dare you?! Okay?

ANOTHER GUY: What?!

ONE GUY: That's it. I'm washing my hands of this thing. Okay?

ANOTHER GUY: That's what?

ONE GUY: That's it. That's all I'm gonna to say about this over here. I can't get anywhere with this thing. What do you want, my blood? Here, bleed me dry. Go ahead. What are you waiting for? Get out your jar of leeches and we'll do the sixteenth century thing over here in the barber's chair. You strap me down and then bleed me to death like the butcher we all know you really are. Is that what you want over here? Go ahead. Expel the foul humours from my broken body and then drag my wilted corpse behind your fuckin' chariot. What are you waiting for anyway? An invitation?

ANOTHER GUY: I'm gonna say one thing over here—

ONE GUY: What? What? What are you gonna say? Enlighten me, okay? Dazzle me with your footwork, but don't ask me another question or you're gonna give me an absolutely fatal stroke over here.

ANOTHER GUY: I only have one question, all right? I'm gonna say this one thing and then I'm not gonna say anything else. Okay? And it's gonna get very quiet in here because I'm not gonna be talking any more. And if there is any talking going on in here, it's going to be your own private fuckin' musings to yourself with me not here. Because I'm not gonna stay here. I'm gonna be gone from here in some other place where you're not gonna be. Okay? Because I'm tired of your shit. I'm tired of the way you let this woman get over on you like she's the Queen of Sheba and you're some kind of dirtbag who just walked in off the street with no agenda to grovel on the floor and get your nose rubbed raw on her stylish spiked high-heel shoes. She's apparently sayin' things to the Big Guy about you behind your back but not out of earshot. All right? Here's the question. Are you going to let this woman affect the way the Big Guy thinks of you? Or the way you think of the Big Guy? Okay? I want you to think for a second before you reply or retort with a question. And don't say the first or the second thing that pops into your head. Say the third thing. All right? Chew on it for a little while if that's not asking too much.

ONE GUY: Wait a minute. Wait. You want the short answer or the long answer? What do you want over here?

ANOTHER GUY: No, no, don't do that. Stop, okay? That's the first thing that popped into your head. I'm askin' you very politely not to do this to me here for once in your life. Okay?

ONE GUY: But—

ANOTHER GUY: No. (*They both kneel*) No. Please don't start this again.

ONE GUY: I'm not gonna address that question without some clarification over here. And I'm gonna tell you why in great detail so there's no fuckin' confusion or category mistake between us. 'Cause I like you and I wouldn't want a thing like that of all things to come between us. Okay? So I'm gonna take you through this slowly so there's no question and—

ANOTHER GUY: I knew it. I knew it. I knew you couldn't resist doing this thing again you're doing over here.

ONE GUY: Who is the Big Guy anyway? This is the thing I wanted you to clarify for me if it's not gonna be a problem for you in this kind of situation over here.

ANOTHER GUY: A problem? A problem? You most definitely implied to me that you knew who the Big Guy was. If someone's having a problem here, it's you, all right? You're having a bad thing with this kind of slippery slope argument over here because you can't answer the question at hand.

ONE GUY: But I can see by the way that you're fidgeting that you don't know the answer to the big question about you know who.

ANOTHER GUY: I don't care about that question right now!

ONE GUY: Yes you do, but you're avoiding it because it dwarfs the limited faculties you have at your disposal over here, okay?

ANOTHER GUY: Who's avoiding what? That's what I want to know.

ONE GUY: Exactly.

(*They stand*)

ANOTHER GUY: How would you know?

ONE GUY: I had an idea about it. Why won't you answer the question?

ANOTHER GUY: Because of the context in which you asked me that question. You asked me that question under false pretenses of the worst kind.

(*They walk slowly downstage side by side*)

ANOTHER GUY: You ask the big question to avoid the little. You always ask the big to avoid the little.

ONE GUY: I ask the big to avoid the—

ANOTHER GUY: Little . . .

ONE GUY: The big? It's not that big. You want big? I'll show you big—

ANOTHER GUY: 'Cause you can't deal with the little. See?

ONE GUY: And what about the middle?

(*They stop, facing the audience*)

ANOTHER GUY: There is no middle. With you it's always the big to avoid the little.

(*They both stick out their tongues and take communion*)

ONE GUY: Chicken—

ANOTHER GUY: Little.

ONE GUY: Big chicken—

ANOTHER GUY: Little.

ONE GUY: The heavens are—

ANOTHER GUY: Falling down.

ONE GUY: On our heads.

ANOTHER GUY: Woe unto us . . . over here.

MACCHINISTA   *by John Poglinco*

For Susan Skoog

Characters:

Frank—A young man.

Unc—An old man.

Time: Night

Setting: A garage in a city

There is a large engine sitting on a rolling cart center stage. One large wrench lies next to it. Frank wears grease-covered overalls with no shirt underneath. He grunts and strains to loosen a bolt from the engine with a second, even larger wrench. He can't budge it. He tries it from a new position and pulls even harder. He falls to the floor. He hits the engine with the wrench.

FRANK: You mother! You motherfuckin' metal fuckin' steel piece of tin! I'll kill you!

(Exhausted, he lies down on top of the engine. Frank drops the wrench to the floor. There is a long silence)

(Unc enters. He is dressed the same as Frank. He moistens a stogie with his pucker)

UNC: What the hell's going on here?!

(Frank jumps up)

FRANK: Nothing . . .

UNC: You wanna hump engines, go to the goddamn junkyard and blow a freakin' gasket. This is a place of business and I'm in here bustin' my guy-oons trying to teach you something.

FRANK: I couldn't fix it, Unc.

UNC: What am I gonna do with you? You're killin' me. Bosses' breathin' down my neck. I ask the family for help and my sister, may she rest in peace, sends me you, the original sad sack a' shit.

FRANK: I was tryin' all night. I couldn't get no grip.

UNC: Can't fix it, huh?

FRANK: No, I can't, Unc.

UNC: Can't get no grip?

FRANK: It ain't easy.

UNC: You're having difficulties?

FRANK: One could say that.

(*Unc smacks Frank in the back of the head*)

UNC: One could also say that you're a stunade who's thick in the head who ain't got no faculties!

FRANK: I got lotsa' faculties. I can picture things. I can picture things that ain't here.

UNC: Like?

FRANK: Like . . . Ma. Like . . . a dog driving a go-cart and wearing a helmet. Like the girls on that naked calendar you got hanging in the office coming to life and helping me fix cars. Like a white flying horse going out fast over rooftops, and hovering at windows talking to all the lonely people in apartments, flying away, and then winning big at Belmont.

UNC: Frankie, you gotta stop that kind of thinking. It ain't leading you nowhere.

FRANK: What if we didn't have to work in this pit? What if we didn't have to be dirty all the time? What if—

UNC: "What ifs" ain't allowed in this work area. "What ifs" make the boss nervous. "What ifs" cause dreaming. "What ifs" cause heart diseases. "What ifs" encourage what-do-ya'-call . . . entering the freakin' unchartered realms of speculative metaphysics.

FRANK: Say what?

UNC: No! What! Ifs! That's what sunk Gottfried Wilhelm Leibniz and the rest of them goddamn dreamers.

FRANK: Was Gottfried Wilhelm Leibniz Italian like us?

UNC: Uh . . . yeah. They was all Italian, them guys. Said somethin' 'bout we live in the best of all possible worlds.

FRANK: It don't feel like no best possible world.

(*There is a long silence*)

UNC: I know. That'll wear off with time.

FRANK: Show me how to do something, Unc. Please. Show me how to do anything.

UNC: When I was your age I could get a handle on a machine like this and ones even bigger. I could get a fix on an engine like this with my empirical tools, then strap the mother to my hairy back and climb ten flights up to an ivory tower with one thumb tied behind me and the other one stickin' up my ass.

FRANK: Yeah, you already told me what you used to do. What can you do now, Unc?

UNC: Okay, wise ass. You do like this. Keep your eyes open.

(*Unc attacks the engine in a frenzy, wrenching off nuts and bolts. Pieces of metal fly left and right*)

UNC: Then you break it down like this . . .

FRANK: Wow, Unc! You're cookin'!

UNC: Fuckin' A, kid!

FRANK: How do you do it?

UNC: I just do like this and the jaws of my wrench grab it, break it down, and lay it all out so's we can apprehend it.

FRANK: The wrench grabs it?

UNC: Whatever you can't hold on to! See?!

FRANK: And . . . and then what happens?

UNC: Look what I'm doing over here! I use my critical leverage and figure out the fucking situation!

FRANK: And the wrench is a jaw?

UNC: Two poles! Equal pressure! Opposing forces! Contradiction for chrissakes!

FRANK: And what's in the middle?

(*Unc stops and clutches his side. He staggers and leans on the engine*)

UNC: What do you think's in the freakin' middle?! Synthesis! (*Beat*) Oh, sweet Jesus, Mary, Joseph, and them three guys on the camels.

(*Unc slides on to the floor. Frank runs to his side*)

FRANK: Unc, what's wrong?

UNC: My heart . . . you threw a wrench into my broken heart.

FRANK: I'm sorry. I didn't mean to, Unc. I was trying. I was really trying to learn.

UNC: Get offa' me! I need some air over here!

FRANK: But . . . but you're sick.

UNC: I made a mistake when I promised your mother that I could teach you how to get a grip and see what's for real. Look at you! You ain't even breakin' a sweat and you got me dancin' a goddamn jig over here. You're killing me.

FRANK: Don't make talk like that, Unc.

UNC: Come here. (*Frank moves closer*) Come closer. Let me whisper something cryptic in your ear in a dialect you probably never heard before.

FRANK: How come with you everything's in secret code I can't understand? How come your whole world is this engine?! How come we can't go outside?!

UNC: Kiss me, Frank. My heart's crappin' out. This could be *it.*

FRANK: It? What's it?

UNC: *It!* It's . . . *not.*

FRANK: Not what?

UNC: No! Not "not what"! Just *not!*

FRANK: You mean . . . "what-not?"

UNC: No, not "what-not." "What-not's" casual. "What-not's" like whatever or etc. There's nothing casual about *not.*

FRANK: What's *not?*

UNC: *Not's* the big blackout. *Not's* when the prime mover moves out and

leaves no forwarding address. Return to sender. An infinity of floating
zeros hoverin' like bubbles when you're passed out drunk with your fly
open at a champagne wedding. Aluf null. The old sideways eight. Not's
when the whale shits Jonah under the ice floes in the Arctic Ocean and
nobody ever writes about it. The end. Fine. Termine. Estremita. Morte.
Trapasso. So kiss me. Da me un bacio.

FRANK: What do ya' mean, like a peck on the cheek?

UNC: A nephew's kiss of respect for an uncle who's on his way out because
you're killin' me over here the way you broke my heart with your thick
head that is like a brick wall that cannot be penetrated by human beings.

FRANK: I know I'm thick, Unc. Just don't leave me like this.

(*Frank moves in to kiss Unc*)

UNC: Don't kiss me. Kiss my wrench. (*Frank grimaces and kisses Unc's
wrench*) Hold still, Frankie.

FRANK: Why?

UNC: 'Cause I said so. (*Unc clasps the wrench around Frank's nose*) Okay,
now show me your pearly whites.

FRANK (*smiling*): Like this?

UNC: Yeah . . .

(*Unc slowly twists and manipulates Frank's nose*)

FRANK: That don't feel so good, Unc.

UNC: I'm tryin' to teach you somethin' for chrissakes! (*Beat*) Now say
"uncle."

FRANK: Uncle . . .

(*Unc releases Frank*)

UNC: Go to it, kid.

(*Frank slowly and tentatively starts to dismantle the engine*)

FRANK: Like this?

UNC: Yeah, but more careful. Use what I taught you. Take the long view. Break it down. Spread it all out. Get your head around it. Don't hold nothin' back. Look for the opposites. Use the opposites to hold on. See what's inside, flip it over, then turn it in on itself, and then turn it inside out. Continual resolution with a spiral of new contradictions inside.

FRANK: I'm tryin' to do my best over here.

UNC: That ain't good enough, Frankie.

FRANK: I'll go slow until I get it right.

UNC: Nobody ever gets it right exactly 'cause there's always new wrinkles that show up. Just don't forget to use the right tools. Use your wrench to get a grip. You use the black and the white to hold on to the gray. You see a clam and a tomato, and you can be damn sure there's gonna be a clam-ato in the immediate area. You lean on being and non-being to grasp be-coming. You start with an oyster on one hand and a majorette on the other and—

FRANK: This helps you to picture an oysterette?!

UNC: Right, kid. Now your hands are tied. You're exhausted. You can't feed your family. You got the new boss bustin' your hump up here and you got your valid grievances against this boss down here. So you—

FRANK: You kill the bosses' wife and kids?!

UNC: No, you can't use the bosses' tools to dismantle the bosses' house. My heart, it's burning up. You gotta use your faculties, Frank . . . you see what I'm sayin'?

(*Unc suddenly goes limp and hangs his head down against his chest. He stops breathing*)

FRANK: I think I got the picture, Unc. Hey, Unc. What was that you was sayin' about burning down the bosses' house? Unc? (*Frank stares at Unc, horrified*)

(*Blackout.*)

AN INTERVIEW WITH JON POGLINCO, *author of* Over Here *and* Macchinista

What first prompted you to write plays?
I tried writing novels but I couldn't do it. Too many words, not enough action. So I wrote my first play about twelve years ago. It was about construction workers, and I was working construction at the time. It seemed like the perfect medium to capture the voices of people, as opposed to the descriptions a novelist would write.

What is the most important thing for you in writing a play?
The most essential, most basic idea behind putting something on stage is narrative structure. Telling a story is the most important thing, unless you're a genius and you can break the structure to create a tour de force.

What do you think about the state of theater in the U.S. today?
A lot of people write plays that are so-called avant garde, but I don't get a sense that the writers are trying to communicate something human to me. They're just kind of jerking off. I didn't gravitate to theater for the experience of hearing nice words. It's to communicate something—and to have something communicated to me when I'm in the audience.

Dramatically, what were you aiming to do with *Over Here*?
With *Over Here* I was trying to show the internal lives of working-class people. They have thinking lives, even if they're not educated or have been de-educated by the so-called educational system. In the play, these too goombahs are having a philosophical discussion in church about a woman's ass. They're grappling with concrete ideas in philosophical terms.

What about "Macchinista"?
People ponder the world, even people who don't have educations and haven't been encouraged to ponder it. They grapple with ideas they don't understand, can't understand—but want to understand. It's pretty much the human condition; we're pretty primitive, all people. And we can see that more in a character who is a knucklehead, but who nonetheless wants to understand the mysteries of the universe—God. That's really who we all are. I was also trying to understand my father in that play.

Given the minimal financial rewards for writing for the stage, why do you do it?

It's immediate, irrevocable in time and space. You can't fake it on stage.

Is there any advice you would give to aspiring playwrights?

Don't bore the audience. Your job is to hurl emotion at them. That's your first job. They have to feel things, otherwise it's all intellectual.

SAUCY PAPER   *By Daniel Aukin*

The sounds of a street in a small town in northern Italy, just off a piazza: distant birds chirping, far off traffic. It is the middle of a hot day. Glaring lights come up on an outdoor cafe area. Very bare bones: Two tables, stage left and right, equidistant from each other; a far upstage center doorway (preferably a swinging door) leads into the cafe interior. Each table has two chairs.

Sitting at the stage right table is a male tourist: Brian Wu, he could be any-where from twenty-five to forty-five years old. He is wearing conspicuously generic American tourist garb: broad-rimmed sun hat, zinc-creamed nose, small travel pouch, and money belt. He has a tall glass of iced water on the table which he sips carefully and intermittently.

The Waiter, formally dressed with a folded towel over one arm and a tray under the other, marches out from the doorway to far downstage left. He lights a cigarette, takes five quick puffs, stamps it out and heads back to the upstage door.

A twenty-something female backpacker, Monica, enters from stage left, carrying a plastic bottle of water in her hand. Seeing her, the waiter slows down and elects to stay outside, standing to one side of the upstage door.

Monica comes to a stop downstage left, unhitches her pack and puts it on the ground. She takes a sip from the bottle.

At precisely the same time, Brian, watching her intently, takes a sip from his glass of water.

The lights dim for a second and return to full brightness.

Monica wipes her brow.

She pulls a folded map from her pack.

She turns to look at the empty café table and then turns back.

She opens up a section of the fold-out map and compares it to where she is. A fly comes near the map and she vaguely swats it away.

She takes four paces stage right and, shielding her eyes with her arm, looks off to a distant landmark.

She brings the water bottle to her lips and almost *drinks from it.*

Brian stares at her intently, his glass of water in hand. She takes four steps stage left back to where she first stopped. She returns the map to the pack.

The waiter walks downstage and wipes the stage left table with a cloth.

Suddenly, the waiter notices that Brian is staring intently at Monica. The waiter does a double-take to Monica and then Brian. The waiter makes a rush for Monica. Just then both Monica and Brian sip from their drinks.

The lights dim.

The waiter stops a yard short of pouncing on Monica. He stops abruptly, unsure what he was about to do. His eyes begin to blink mechanically. Brian and Monica's eyes are also blinking. The waiter returns to his upstage position by the doorway.

The lights return to full brightness. All the eyes return to normal.

Monica wipes her brow.

She pulls a folded map from her pack.

She turns to look at the empty cafe table and then turns back.

She opens up a section of the fold-out map and compares it to where she is. A fly comes near the map and she vaguely swats it away.

She takes four paces stage right and, shielding her eyes with her arm, looks off to a distant landmark.

She brings the water bottle to her lips and almost *drinks from it.*

Brian stares at her intently, his glass of water in hand. She takes four steps stage left back to where she first stopped. She returns the map to the pack.

The waiter walks downstage and wipes the stage left table with a cloth.

Suddenly, the waiter notices that Brian is staring intently at Monica. The waiter does a double-take to Monica and then Brian. The waiter makes a rush for Monica. Just then both Monica and Brian sip from their drinks.

The waiter stops a yard short of pouncing on Monica. He stops abruptly, unsure what he was about to do. His eyes begin to blink mechanically. Brian and Monica's eyes are also blinking. The waiter returns to his upstage position by the doorway.

The lights return to full brightness. All the eyes return to normal.

Monica wipes her brow.

BRIAN (*voice over*): Breathe slowly. (*Monica pulls a folded map from her pack*) Breathe slowly.

MONICA (*voice over*): I'm waiting for Georg. This doesn't sound like Georg. (*Monica turns to look at the cafe table and then turns back*)

BRIAN (*voice over*): It's me it's me this is so exciting I'm not Georg I'm Brian Wu I'm telesending holy Vishnu don't worry he can't hear us.

(*She opens up a section of the fold-out map and compares it to where she is. A fly comes near the map and she vaguely swats it away*)

It doesn't matter you will realize it shortly necessary confusion I ask that you listen a time hiccup you are an operative working in deep cover for Prestigious Systems—(*Monica takes four paces stage right and, shielding her eyes with her arm, looks to a distant landmark*)—and Warehousing Prestigious Systems and Warehousing a front for an interplanetary spatial relations conglomerate and market research concern time hiccup a safe space plastic fields this is all too much for you pay attention— (*Holding the water bottle in her free hand she* almost *drinks from it*)— who are you prior training as a Ninsi master of Subtle-istics you the last survivor of Ninsi dynasty rest of colony killed in attack on daytrip to petting zoo this makes you especially excellent only one left for calculating

space/purchase equations essential to perceived success within Prestigious so our competitor Lorcal Systems got wind . . . (*Brian stares at
her, his glass of water in hand. She takes four steps stage left back to
where she first stopped. She returns the map to the pack*) . . . and your
personality was instantly Selwyn-Lumped special order by Prestigious
top brass this is the news lady this is the news you're living with an alternate persona template a safety precaution to protect you from ESPER a
mercenary telepath/abduction unit bent on extracting your special spatial
skills hired by hired by hired by Lorcal our competitor—(*The waiter
walks downstage and wipes the empty table with a cloth*)—there he is
that's their agent one more second you'd be brain stew in one of their
labs—they run account for Handi-snacks a blatant rip-off of the Prestigious' account for Oaty Roll'Ems so we hid you inside yourself under
radar of their mentalistics and mind rape technicololgy capice they plan
on abduction we plan on saving you . . .

(*Suddenly, the waiter notices that Brian is staring intently at Monica. The
waiter does a double-take to Monica and then Brian. The waiter makes a
rush for Monica. Just then both Monica and Brian sip from their drinks.*

The waiter stops a yard short of pouncing on Monica.

The lights dim)

Will you listen to me what I have to tell you is very important you equals
Monica Willcox born 12.23.49 broke up with boyfriend two weeks ago am I
right or am I right this is all implanted all implanted to protect you from yourself we're inside a time hiccup very unstable did I say that send that I mean already well your only hope to buy the space/time necessary to get you out of
this jam alter plastified fields of intention using Ninsi training . . .

(*As before, the waiter has stopped abruptly, a yard from Monica. Unsure
what he was about to do. His eyes begin to blink mechanically*)

MONICA (*voice over*): I don't know what you're talking about. Who the
fuck are you?

BRIAN (*voice over*): Good if you did I would be worried quick here read
this quick.

(*With great effort, while all of them are blinking, Brian makes his way over to Monica as if the air between them is sludge. He puts a newspaper in her hands and returns to his seat)*

MONICA (*voice over*): Dear E.N.: I happen to believe that in most cases . . . try to analyze how realistic my fears are . . . based on reality . . . blah blah blah . . . try overcoming your self pity by taking some positive action . . . yada yada yada . . . if you start taking charge of your thoughts, you will find that you can also improve your self-esteem . . . this isn't doing anything for me I'm afraid.

BRIAN (*voice over*): Again.

(The waiter returns to his upstage position by the doorway. His walking has taken on a strange lopsidedness)

MONICA (*voice over*): Let's see . . . uh huh . . . if you start taking charge of your thoughts . . . you will find . . . no. Nothing.

(The lights return to full brightness. All the eyes return to normal)

BRIAN (*voice over*): This isn't working right damn fuck me sideways Dear Abby is the key we installed to release the Selwyn-Lumping lock your only hope damn that Myrna Ng!

(Monica wipes her brow)

MONICA: Over-come. (*Both waiter and Brian body-twitch as she says this*) Over-come.

(Both waiter and Brian body-twitch again)

BRIAN (*voice over*): Wonderful that's it that's it easy now it's starting loop borders stay in place but intention fields plastify . . .

MONICA (*voice over*): I'm Abigail Randolph daughter of Mercy Randolph III. On my oh my oh my it's all . . . it's all so very so very . . .

(Monica gags as if she is about to be sick. Then, she speaks aloud for the first time, an uncontrolled torrent—at the same time, she goes through the motions of looking through her purse, considering the empty cafe table and then closing the purse and putting it back in the pack)

MONICA: Saucy paper saucy paper saucy paper saucy paper saucy paper saucy paper saucy paper saucy paper saucy paper saucy paper saucy paper saucy paper saucy paper saucy paper saucy paper saucy paper *(The waiter's left arm begins to windmill round and round, faster and faster. She makes the motion of opening up a section of the fold-out map but has no map in her hands. She compares it to where she is. She swats at a fly)* Dear me a lady like a peanut salad sal-ad sal-ad leaving leaving leaving a human not not not like telephone like our saviors savor snacks and squared root of going it blindside river stylee *(She takes four paces stage right and looks to a distant landmark. Monica almost drinks from the water bottle)*

BRIAN *(voice over)*: Okay that's great. Now here's what must happen. You must sufficiently alter the agent's intention field so that he has no idea of jaunting you off as was his plan.

(Over the following dialogue Monica manipulates Brian and the Waiter's actions more and more, something like a jazz-improvisation. Each set of words sets off a corresponding movement in Brian and the Waiter, deviating from the looping sequence they otherwise feel compelled to repeat. The movements can stretch from baroque mutations to small gestural curlicues)

MONICA *(voice over, bold indicates normal speech)*	**BRIAN** *(voice over)*:	*(Brian stares at her, his glass of water in hand)*
Haste vase paste a region	We must re-enter consensual time that is storming the cup that is storming the cup shit I'm repeating myself which means which means which means which means which means which means which means which means which means which means which means which means	*(He is standing. He sprinkles some of the water from his glass onto his head)*
for soil erosion erosion corpuscle sonata largesse meander lemonscented a hula groove dula wappidy		
ferpid smoth a langor train like so called like so called greener than thou a frown a curcacedous livacious	which means which means which means which means which means which means which means which means	*(Monica takes four steps stage left back to where she first stopped. She waves at the roving fly again. Brian and Waiter start*

spooning new new
flew haste vase
paste a region for
soil erosion erosion
corpuscle sonata
largesse meander
lemonscented

a hula groove dula
wappidy ferpid
smoth a langor train
like so called like
so called greener
than thou a frown a
curvaceous liva-
cious spooning a
new new flew

a torpedo mover
smooth the new
grocery like a high
a rivulet a corner-
stone so new a flute
ton ton stewy wis-
dom over the

hillock bo billock si
fi li ho nillock

which means which
means which means
which means which
means which means
which means which
means which means
which means which
means which means
which means which
means which means
which means which
means which means
which means which
means which means

which means which
means which
means which
means which
means extreme

concentration on
last thing you were
thinking of doing
smallest smallest
smallest smallest
smallest smallest
smallest smallest
smallest smallest
smallest smallest
thing just as loop-
ing hiccup began
you remember?

*to move more and
more strangely)*

*(She returns the map
to the pack)*

*(The waiter walks
downstage and wipes
the stage left table
with a cloth)*

*(The wiping gesture
can get larger and
larger, out of control)*

*(As before, the waiter
suddenly notices that
Brian is staring in-
tently at Monica)*

*(The waiter does a
double-take to Mon-
ica and then Brian.
The double take be-
comes part of a
dance—"the Itch," a
new version of "the
Funky Chicken"—
that Brian and the
waiter do under Mon-
ica's verbal control)*

I'm not sure. I was waiting for Georg.

Rorification loudness the bomb squad a dooby squa squa ma raidy a loovey hunk a cheshire in my cap a loovey hunk a cheshire in my cap a loovey hunk a cheshire in my cap a loovey hunk a cheshire in my cap a loovey hunk a cheshire in my cap

Don't think a Ninsi goes past thinking go to the very next thing just before you drink think the thing you were going to do think before you drink

Forget that too big too big don't think about it

(Brian and Waiter's version of "the Itch" gets more and more elaborate)

(However, within this new movement we also see the waiter struggling with the impulse to pounce on Monica)

Waiting for a friend.

I was coming to make a call maybe

Don't think it!

For your own sake I hope not.

(The waiter's resolve strengthens as he desperately battles to be free of the dance so that he can get Monica)

Am I going to remember who I am?

Lamdy heh heh I saucy paper this ya big lummox!

(The waiter is in pounce position)

(The waiter makes a rush for Monica. They are all in the same position they are always in at the end of the loop of action. Just then both Monica and Brian sip from their drinks)

(A return to linear time. The sound of chirping birds and distant traffic. The waiter, instead of pouncing on Monica, turns and swats a fly on the

table he had been cleaning. At the same time, Brian and Monica put their hands to their necks as if they had each been bitten on the neck. The waiter pinches the dead bug off the table and wipes the surface down. Monica sighs)

(Black)

INTERVIEW WITH DANIEL AUKIN, author of Saucy Paper and Artistic Director of Soho Repertory Theatre

Tell us something about your introduction to theater.

When I was young, both my parents were in the business: my father an artistic director of a theater in London, and my mother a director (Nancy Meckler of Shared Experience). The first show I remember seeing was *Kiss Me Kate*, directed by my mother. All her work had a big impact on me. Also, a performance group that my father produced a number of times—The People Show. The People Show work without a director, and build plays together that have this seemingly wild, uncontrolled quality—but really they're incredibly controlled and specific.

What first prompted you to write plays?

The first play I wrote was in college, with Steve Moore (now of Physical Plant Theater in Austin, Texas). I was inspired by reading an interview with Richard Foreman. I'd never seen any of Foreman's plays at that time, but I found what he said about theater incredibly articulate and full of common sense—and radical.

What is your professional background as a playwright?

I come to writing through directing. I don't really consider myself a playwright. For one of my full-length plays, I didn't set pen to paper until I'd worked with two actors for nine months generating the show. That's my point of entry.

What were you aiming to do with *Saucy Paper*?

I had an idea of a certain sequence of movement that I wanted to see on stage. And then I tried to find the words to help give a narrative context to that first impulse.

Where do you situate theater in mainstream American culture?

Because theater is a live medium and the means of distribution are necessarily local for all but the biggest touring shows, there's a lot of exciting work that fails to reach a wide audience. For example, there might well be a play with a sensibility like *South Park* or *Pee Wee's Playhouse* that would never find an audience larger than a midnight crowd in a downtown space. That same sensibility distributed on cable becomes a phenomenon.

Given the minimal financial rewards for working in the theater, why do you do it?

It's always going to be more sensible not to work in the theater, but there's something unique to the experience of an astonishing theatrical work. Theater asks so much of you as an audience member. When it soars, it lifts you in a way that other mediums do not.

ICEBOX *by J.R. Riddick*

Lights up. Massive brick. Johnny-pump. Asphalt. Large curb. Clive etches skelley court with neon-green chalk while thumbing milktop. Pauses. Sits on edge of curb. Tangiers enters from stage right.

TANGIERS: Hot day, biyatch . . .

CLIVE (*looking the other way and giving Tangiers the finger*): I love you too biyatch . . .

TANGIERS: Leaving tomorrow?

CLIVE: Today, yo . . . today . . .

TANGIERS (*aghast*): True that, partner? What is up with mama Gregory, kid? She wants you out the house like yesterday . . .

(*Sound of woman's voice offstage. Loud. Hoarse. Sharp and sassy*)

WOMAN (*offstage*): Pregnant with a large cucumber at age forty-two. Forty-two. Yes. In a particular way. A vicious tearing fizzing my pussy . . . geechie ma was in love with a caramel-type, coated, green-laced musician from the Carolinas. Shit, the north one. Where they graze Uncle Ben's rice. He was white. With the flair and the coins. Not an ungrateful white. He was white white white white white. His whiteness never dispossessed my feared representation. Anyway, I gave him sweet mangoes of love. Passion fruit-tay. The promissory note was my cucumber baby . . . sour . . .

TANGIERS: Shut up! Shut up! Shut the fuck up! (*To Clive*) Tired of her yappin' her gums like that.

CLIVE: Tangiers, she didn't do anything to you . . .

TANGIERS: I can't sleep at night with that damn racket man. A brother gotta go to work in the mornings. Whattup with that Clive?

CLIVE: You don't have a job. You never had a job. When was the last time your lazy ass got a job?

TANGIERS: Today, I'm your damn counselor. Tell me, what's the malady, kid?

CLIVE: My moms brought me a ticket to leave to Boston a day early. I confronted her, like bladdow! Moms whats'up, and she gives me the shimmy about getting myself prepared for the new school year. I hate Deerfield. Mad constricting. No haircut, no music, no pussy . . . No pussy in Massachusetts. I'd rather be on death row.

TANGIERS: You gotta let her know, brother. Tell her you're not happy there. Yo, when my moms act the fool sometime, you know, I have to set things straight with her . . .

CLIVE: Yo Tangiers, you moms died of sugar in '82. Block party. Chaka jumped from the welfare hotel across the street. That block party.

(*Silence. Tangiers stares at Clive blankly. Miffed*)

TANGIERS: You are afraid. I have dilemmas. (*Tangiers laughs sardonically. Clive sighs heavily*)

WOMAN (*offstage*): Lucy let lots of nasty negroes lavish lovingly with lime tongues on her body. Lucy little sister was a sitter for Mr. Tyler on Broadway. Shhhhhh! We listened to Lavern Baker on our sparkling neon and gold record player. Oh, law'd have mercy, Lucy fell in love with Mr. Onett Walker Tyler, the doomed employer. Tyler was quarteroon but he was a full bastard nevertheless. Her baby boy became a box key. Spring from the ghetto I say. Spring forth, spring out, spring deep, spring, spring away. Warm day, they took my boy. Lucy latched onto my baby. Lucy stole my bubbling baby's hot water.

(*Tangiers stands up. Huffs upon the street. Turns around*)

TANGIERS: Your baby's dead. He's gone. You will never see him again. The good times has rolled, missy. Shut the hell up!

(*Clive motions with his milk top towards an erratic Tangiers*)

CLIVE: Leave the woman alone. Her mind's off-the-wall. Straight-no-chaser gone.

TANGIERS: One of these days, I'mma kill that bitch. God as my word. Talking about things that don't make no goddamn sense whatsoever. When I lay awake at night, I want to hear sounds of gunshots and domestic moanings. Not some shriveled-up geeche bitch with a penchant for tall tales.

CLIVE: Don't you think I hear it? Yes, we all do. Practically everyone on a five-mile radius can hear her. She needs someone to talk to. The greatest need of a human being is to have their presence affirmed. (*Clive hikes the milk top on the ground before them*) Let's play our last game of skelley before I become pussyless in Massachusetts . . .

(*Silence. Tangiers pulls out a large mayonnaise top. Hikes it onto the floor*)

TANGIERS: My bad, my bad Clive Gregory. This is your day. I have a glutton of misforgetness . . .

CLIVE: You got that big-ass skelley top. You mind is not that gone yet! Cheating ass . . . (*As they play on the court, he gets down on his knees and shoots his milktop at the large mayonnaise top*) I can't wait to go back up to Massachusetts. I can have all the chocolate chip ice-cream I want. Play skell-zee in the cafeterias all night. Lounge around the dorms with my leopard print boxers and play Sega Genesis on weekends. The prize—to be away from all of your crap.

(*Tangiers gets on his knees and is ready to shoot his large top*)

TANGIERS: Look out for the forthcoming, yo. This is the mammoth bo-hemmoth, baby.

(*Tangiers goes to shoot his top towards Clive's. As he does, the sudden burst of noise sends his top askew*)

WOMAN (*offstage*): Bombs. Bombs and Disappointment. A novel I wrote in high school. Got me on the honor rolls. Shucks. A masterpiece that would easily segueway into Yale status. No body, no children. Bombs blew up my living room. I could bend and stretch my mind twenty-seven different ways for cover and counterattack. The essay. Classification of netherworld happy folk: Does poverty make a subject have the where-withal to access happiness? Crafted an epilogue for my hard-earned epitaph . . . When you know my life,/What do you know?/When you know my womanhood,/What do you really know?/When you know my soul,/What can you truly know?/My self, in deed, with keepings, untold . . .

(*An enraged Tangiers takes large top and flings it off in the distance*)

CLIVE: Mama says anger will get you nowhere . . .

TANGIERS: She's messing up my game. She's always fucked up my skel-ley game. This is our last game. Not fair.

(*Clive picks up his milk top and sits back on the curb*)

CLIVE: We can always play spades.

TANGIERS: Fuck spades. Fuck you.

CLIVE: Fuck you too. I gotta stop cursing.

TANGIERS: Cursing helps me keep the world in check. Why do you do it?

CLIVE: Cause you do it, punk. I look up to you, big bro biyatch. See, where did that come from?

(*Tangiers laughs softly. Clive joins in. They laugh together. They sit on the curb*)

WOMAN (*offstage*): There is nothing funny. There's nothing funny. Laugh all you want. You're not free from yourself. Laugh. Laugh all you wish. You can never hide from what is there. I don't see anything funny. Forging a glow doesn't make it so. I didn't give you two permission to laugh at me. Do you know who I am?

TANGIERS: What the fuck now? I'll play along . . . who are you today? Let me guess, Angela Davis . . . no, no, how about Lady Queen Isabella and we are who, the servants, right? Don't be ashamed to say it. Shit, once you say it, we obey it!!!

(*Tangiers and Clive bow down in mock fashion and laugh hysterically*)

WOMAN (*offstage*): The last time I laughed was on a feelgood August afternoon. Nineteen eighty-seven. When Ms. Gregory died.

TANGIERS: Yo Clive, she's talking about your moms. Don't let her talk about your moms like that.

(*Tangiers nudges Clive to react. Clive shakes his head. Slight smile*)

CLIVE: Hey, hey, hey, my mother did not die. It was his mother. You got the two mamas mixed up. I wish my moms was gone. I wouldn't have to leave, ya' know . . .

TANGIERS: You're a flake, you know that don'tcha?

CLIVE: Take after your moms . . .

(*Tangiers throws a blow at Clive. Strikes him on the ground. Silence. Clive seethes in disgust. Blood. Clive jumps on Tangiers. They struggle in the street. The woman appears upstage of the battling duo. Tattered long off-white gown. Misty eyed. She scans the activity*)

WOMAN: I placed the eye on the tray. Covered it with water lettuce. Yes, it was watery, mouth watery. Crying water fills the hopeful cup. Deep sorrow with the eye. The eye assaults my dreams with negative queries from everybody's and everybody else's concerns. Waging battles. Unlatching the visceral wars. The dust that surrounds the eye settle. Particles scratch. Ungraced corneas. I become the eye half-becomed and halfed-beloved. Shut-eyes stumped. I'm always asleep with the eye gone, the other a zealous czar. Ruling history. Back and forth. The eye on the tray is passed on to a fearful space . . .

(*Tangiers shoves Clive up on the brick wall. Clive utters a loud primal grunt. Slides down the wall. Tangiers stands still in exhaustion. Blood covers his clothes. The woman glides over the skelley court. Never taking her eyes off them, she sits downstage center in cautious anticipation*)

CLIVE: I must leave from this god-forsaken place . . .

TANGIERS: Must you? Stay the fuck here. You can always transfer to

some private school here. Could never handle your business publicly.
Like you're someone special. The special chile.

CLIVE: Are you speaking the honest-to-goodness truth or some ghetto
lore?

TANGIERS: How long we've been in the cut together? As long as I can remember? My answer, for good or bad, will not change your life . . .

CLIVE: I respect your opinion. I'm still learning quite callously the reason
why.

(*Tangiers goes over to Clive leaning against the wall. Outstretched hand*)

TANGIERS: 'Cause you love me.

CLIVE: I would bet a fat man that I don't. (*Clive reaches for Tangiers'
hand. Pulled up from the ground. Wipes the blood off his face. Breathes
deeply. Centers himself*) You want something to eat? I've cooked some
chouder. Spam chouder with mama's favorite . . . salad.

TANGIERS: Double nasty, yo. Clive, I'm gonna miss you. No one can
take a beating quite like you.

CLIVE: Thank you brother, thank you. I've been abused by the best.

(*The two hug each other. The woman, who is deliriously pleased, walks towards them. She wraps her arms around them slowly. Clive, who watches
her apprehensively, embraces Tangiers harder*)

WOMAN: I've won five hundred dollars yesterday. Yes, sir. Big money.
Big loads of feelgood fun.

(*Clive breaks away from a despondent Tangiers. Tangiers tries to grab him.
The woman, frightened, moves hurriedly upstage center. Gazes at Clive in
shock*)

CLIVE (*explosive*): I'M LEAVING NOW . . . I CAN'T STAY . . .

TANGIERS: Clive, buddy, not now, we've come this far. Everyone is still
looking at us to do what we have to do . . .

WOMAN: Oh yes. Stopped by the number house and spoke to Johnny. I say, "Johnny mack, slide me a 318 and a 329 for a dollar straight and fifty cents combinated!" Jesus, the man did not double-C a thang, you hear me?

CLIVE: I hear you, yes . . . look at me . . . I can't do this anymore . . . I helped too much . . . I'm used up . . .

WOMAN: Boiling point broke my glass house. I got those numbers from Walona Berry. Story is she found her dead husband's old number slips in his pockets. Dated nineteen thirty-eight. Played them as her played it.

TANGIERS: We gotta play the game, yo. No punking out. We have to . . . no . . . we need to talk to each other. Who else is there to talk to?

CLIVE: Her.

(*Silence*)

TANGIERS: Please, she talks to everybody. Remember what your mother said about getting upset.

CLIVE: I can't bleed anymore for us. I don't have the patience to stay here. I gotta leave. Everyone on the block watching. We've won. Got over once again. We've done all the stories. We've heard all the stories. Tangiers, I wish . . . I wish someone would teach me the game of my life. Very slowly. So I can catch up to myself . . .

(*Clives leaves solemnly stage right. Tangiers stands still in horror, devastated*)

WOMAN: Five hundred dollars. Yep, brought my son a Red Sox jacket. He likes Massachusetts. I say, when he get some Massachusetts money, he can go there anytime he want. Nobody's stopping him. That's fine allright with me cause I'm a strong person. I haven't lived this long being a weakling . . . (*Yells loudly*) Tangiers, you know whom I am? (*Silence*) Tangiers, I see you on the curb next to the handball court. Don't let me embarrass you out there in front of your friends. Do you know who I am? Do you know who I am?

(*Tangiers sits on the curb, exasperated*)

TANGIERS: No, Mama . . . what?

(*The woman outstretches her arms to the sky. Enjoying the moment. Lush, utter peacefulness*)

WOMAN: I am God . . . yes, the simple and the divine . . .

TANGIERS: Sacrificed everything for our lives, I have to love you Mama for that . . .

WOMAN: Yes, yes, shut up for a minute and let me get a word in edgewise . . . Where is your brother? He has to get my salad out of the icebox . . .

(*Tangiers kneels and hugs the woman tightly. Burying his face in her stomach. The woman caresses Tangiers' face*)

WOMAN (*sotto voce*): I am the last hellified mother in black Brooklyn.

(*Silence. Tangiers pulls out a skelley top. Smiles softly*)

TANGIERS: Once you say it, we obey it . . . forever . . .

(*Tangiers throws the skelley top in the distance. Laughs contently. The woman laughs. Sweet and haunting echoed laughter. Lights fade.*)

INTERVIEW WITH J.R. RIDDICK, author of Icebox

How did you begin writing?

From sixth to twelfth grade I wrote serialized stories in these five subject notebooks. I was a fan of soap operas, and I'd have a season finale at the end of the every notebook. It's called *Legacy*. It's thirty-six parts.

What first prompted you to write plays?

When I went to Dartmouth I was going to be an engineering major, but I did want to explore my creative side. A senior I met told me about a black theater organization they had on campus, BUTA (Black Underground Theater and Arts Association). So I auditioned and I got a part. I was a stage manager, I directed a couple of plays, and I eventually became the director of the organization.

At Dartmouth, I wrote *Every 1 is Guilty Until Proven Black*—a one act absurdist play about Black mind police. The point of the play was that nobody lives up to their standards. I did a reading, and I thought it was a serious play, but it ended up being very funny. People were falling out of their seats. Somebody saw it and wanted to do it at Smith College. That was the first time I really got the sense that I was an artist.

Dramatically, what were you aiming to do with *Icebox*?

Icebox wasn't planned. I wrote it straight off the cuff, right after my twenty-fifth birthday. The impetus for it was this woman who lives in the building behind my house in Brooklyn. Every night at two in the morning she screams out random stuff. It turned out my mother knew the woman, and she told me that the woman had problems with her husband. He left her and now her mind is gone. It was really heartbreaking. She had two children. One couldn't take it—he left. The other one stayed and tried to take care of her.

In the play, I wanted to match the rhythm of the mother with the two sons. I work with the different tonal qualities of voice. Sort of like a jazz tune, with the different instruments working together and apart.

What are the biggest influences on your writing?

Pirandello. Arthur Miller. August Wilson. I think all three have a working-class aesthetic, and at the same time their dramatic construction are very academic. They make arguments.

What do you think about the state of theater in the U.S. today?

Being from a working-class background, I don't see too many people like me participating in theater, or going to see it for that matter. I need to bring those people in. They need to see it. Right now I'm starting my own theater company, called Transcendence Entertainment. The theory behind it is that anyone has the power to create art.

Is there any advice you would give to aspiring playwrights?

Be quiet. Writers need the time to think about themselves, and they need to live in the present.

TRUE CONFESSIONS
by Dan Dzindzihashvili

Bare stage with real or imaginary door.

We're in the hallway of an apartment building in Brighton Beach, Brooklyn.

Present. Night.

Misha, 50s, wearing only his boxer shorts and tank top stands in front of the door. He knocks.

MISHA: Hello. Hello. It's your neighbor from next door. Misha Ivanovich Fizetski. Can you open the door?

I need a place to sleep for tonight. I can see your eye through the peep hole. Don't pay any attention to how I'm dressed.

Natasha. My wife. She threw me out of my own home. The fat bitch. I'm sorry. I love her. The fat fuck.

Are you going to let me in? I knocked on everyone else's door. No one seems to be home. You're home. I can see your eye. Do you like my shorts? They're silk. How I need to get some sleep. I can't sleep here in the hallway. This really is funny. I never thought I'd leave Russia and stand outside my neighbor's door begging to sleep on their couch.

Don't you feel sorry for me?

I must say your eye . . . the blue in your eye is very beautiful. Reminds me of the dachas from my childhood by the Black Sea. Are you the man of the house or the Mrs.? I guess you don't feel like talking. I feel like talking a lot. I'll tell you my whole life story if you don't let me in. I have a lot to tell. Not all of it is very interesting.

Can you believe my Natasha threw me out of my house?

When we first got married I used to beat her to a pulp. Then the little twig I married turned into an elephant. She's stronger than me now. I'm the man of the house. I can do whatever I want.

Did you hear the latest news? The pigs over at welfare are cracking down. They want to know why I'm on public assistance. Hello?!!!

These Americans are cheap. The money I get from welfare is not enough. When I sneak off to Atlantic City I lose it in the first hour. $244. That's nothing. These Americans are rich. How much do you get? I am the man of the house. If I go to Atlantic City and gamble our money away . . . it's my right. This is America. A man is free to do as he pleases. BUT THAT COW OF A WIFE WANTS TO BE THE BOSS AND TELL ME THAT I CAN'T GO TO ATLANTIC CITY. My health is not so good, you see.

I met this girl, Svetlana, at the Russian Deli across the street on Brighton and Third Street. She worked in the cheese section. She gave me these boxer shorts. They're silk. Stop looking at me like that or else I'll poke your eyes out. What kind of neighbor are you? I need a bed or a couch.

Svetlana divorced her husband because she was in love with me. But I never left Natasha, MY RUSSIAN BEAR. The bitch.

Let me interrupt myself and tell you about my wife, Natasha. I met her when we were thirteen. We were swimming in the sea and I started doing boy things to myself. She thought that she got pregnant because maybe my sperm would swim through the water and give her a child. We did get a child many years later. A daughter with blue eyes.

Anyway, Svetlana's husband got jealous. He wanted to get even with me. I supposedly took his wife, so he wanted to take something from me. He was bragging in the streets about what he would do to me. He would either kill me or rape my wife . . . but she was too fat or . . . my . . .

He was a man of his word. My own child. She looked at me blankly when she came home. I never saw her after that. She married some Georgian Jew who peddles diamonds on 47th Street. Svetlana's husband thinks he got revenge on me by . . . my own daughter. My daughter wants to hide from me for the rest of her life.

That hog next door . . . she thinks I can stand out here in my underwear all night.

Please, let me in.

(*The door opens and a blanket and pillow come flying out. The door closes*)

I hope you rot in hell.

I'll go to Svetlana and visit her. But how am I going to walk through Brighton Beach in my underwear? Svetlana will think I'm crazy. I'd like to go to her door with a dozen roses wearing an Armani suit.

But if she loves me . . . she'll accept me in my underwear.

(*He lies down on the floor and goes to sleep. Lights fade.*)

INTERVIEW WITH DAN DZINDZIHASHVILI, author of True Confessions

Tell us something about your introduction to theater.

As a bad and funny actor, I made people laugh and cry in Wedekind's *Spring's Awakening* at NYU. I wore S&M gear. Back then I was a size 32 and had muscles. The next semester I was Madame Pace in *Six Characters in Search of an Author* by Pirandello. A straight Jewish boy in drag. I scared the hell out of people. It was a lot of fun, and I quit being a journalist.

What do you think about the state of theater in the U.S. today?

The theater is changing. It's not dying, it's just transforming and adapting to the way the medium is now. Sometimes people say, "this is so much like a sitcom"—or, "why not make it a movie?" A hundred years ago, no one could say that. So the theater is adapting. But simultaneously, people are frustrated because of lack of opportunity.

Dramatically, what were you aiming to do with *True Confessions*?

To make a character that some people would hate into a lovable person that the audience understands. If I had Willy Loman as a father, I would hate him. But when I saw Loman on the stage played by Brian Dennehy, I was in tears. You take a character that not everyone would like, and you make him human.

What is the biggest inspiration for your writing?

Eavesdropping on people's conversations, everywhere I go. Especially older people. I'm interested in older people because as a young person I had to grow up quickly.

Why do you write for the stage?

Because when I'm in the last row of the theater, and the actors are saying my words, and they're making the audience cry and/or laugh, and they clap—that's when I'm happy, because I make them think about their lives, and challenge them. Or confront them.

Is there any advice you would give to aspiring playwrights?

You'll never make money. Don't go in looking for money. Do it because you love it.

CRAWL *by Madelyn Kent*

Montreal. Between three and four o'clock in the morning. On the street, Mikie, 32, waits in heavy rain for a bus. In an effort to stay dry, he pulls his old, soaked jacket over his head.

On the bus, Frances, 20, the only passenger, sits towards the back by a window. She wears a bulky green jacket over a plain dress. Her hair hangs wet–a scavenger caught in the rain.

Mikie boards the bus, flashes a pass from his pocket and walks to the back.

He sits directly behind Frances, on the edge of the seat, and stares at the back of her head.

FRANCES: Smells like shit in here, smells so bad.

MIKIE: Excuse me Miss, you're sitting in my seat.

FRANCES: What?

MIKIE: That's my seat. (*Frances gets up and walks to the other side of the bus. Mikie quickly sits, relieved, but Frances remains standing*) You could sit right down there. (*Frances looks like she could fall any minute*) There are plenty of seats.

FRANCES: Gets so hot. (*Pause*) All the buses in Montreal are overheated. I noticed. Overheatin' and it starts to smell. Everything's cookin' and the rain just makes it worse—all the shit that's comin' from between your toes. Parts of you floating in my nose—

MIKIE: Listen lady, I'm allowed to be here—it's a public bus—

FRANCES: Yeah—not toilet—(*Clutching her stomach*) Oh, shit! (*She bends over in pain, barely looking up*) Where we at?

MIKIE: At the park.

(*Mikie keeps looking out the window*)

FRANCES: Which one?

MIKIE: Outremount.

FRANCES: I hate that park. It used to be my favorite, but then they changed it so much. Where you going?

MIKIE: Nowhere.

FRANCES (*coughs*): What's that?

MIKIE: Nowhere.

FRANCES: Then when you gettin' off?

MIKIE: Downtown.

FRANCES: That's a long time. Two o'clock in the morning, downtown's dead. (*Pause. Mikie says nothing*) I'm getting off at the hospital. See my grandmother.

MIKIE: It's the middle of the night.

FRANCES: It's an emergency.

MIKIE: What hospital you going to?

FRANCES: The Royal Vic.

MIKIE: That's a nice hospital.

FRANCES: I guess you'd think so. You could hang out in the emergency room, it's dry there. You could watch TV, smelling up the whole place.

MIKIE: I've never been inside. From the outside . . . it looks like a castle, up on the mountain.

FRANCES: Looks like a jail.

MIKIE: No it doesn't.

FRANCES: You never been inside. (*Silence. Just the rain*) Why you want to go downtown now? (*Frances doubles over in pain*) Fuck! (*She finally sits, on the back seat. Quickly distracting herself away from the pain*) It's the middle of the night. (*Mikie stares at her*) It's all closed up. (*Mikie stares*) Nothing's there.

MIKIE: I don't sleep.

FRANCES: What?

MIKIE: I don't sleep.

(*Mikie distracts himself, drawing a pattern through the condensation on the window*)

FRANCES: A lot of people who can't sleep, can't sleep cause they did something wrong—

MIKIE: That's not me—

FRANCES: Right when they make a mistake, it gets painted on the backs of their eyelids—

MIKIE: That wouldn't explain why babies can't sleep.

(*Pause*)

FRANCES: What?

MIKIE: Why babies can't sleep. They didn't do anything wrong. (*Beat*) Except if you believe in original sin.

FRANCES: I don't.

MIKIE: No. I don't sleep cause I don't. Too many things going on in this city.

FRANCES: Yeah?

MIKIE: There's a lot going on in this city.

FRANCES: Like what?

MIKIE: Like—like anything.

FRANCES: What do you do instead of sleep?

MIKIE: I got a pass. (*Eagerly taking out a bus pass from his pocket, he holds it out to her. She takes it, looks at it, impressed*) Let's me ride all over the city.

FRANCES: Where did you get that?

MIKIE: Welfare.

FRANCES: Cool.

(*He snatches it back*)

MIKIE: Fuck it man, I ain't gonna sleep. The world's spinning too fast to sleep. (*Pause*) You close your eyes for a second, you miss something. Body just eats you up. And you're . . . thirty-two, something like that.

FRANCES: You're thirty-two? (*Mikie looks out the window*) And you don't have a job?

MIKIE: You can't work if you don't sleep. You don't need a job and you don't need a place either, or a bed if you don't sleep. You see all these poor people around, eh? You see them running to work every day, crammin' on overcrowded buses, working for their house and bed cause of their families.

FRANCES: Yeah.

MIKIE: If you're just up with yourself, taking care of yourself—you don't need any of that.

FRANCES: Otherwise you need everything. All of a sudden. (*Beat*) It just starts out with someone's skin. Someone's skin could smell so good, the taste—the sweat that comes outta people, millions of pores. And then the things that come outta that. Things you never expected.

Things. (*Pause. He looks at her*) Like nothing. (*She stares out the window*)

MIKIE: I saw you. Just before, in the alley.

FRANCES: Huh?

MIKIE: Behind Esplanade.

FRANCES: I wasn't in any alley.

MIKIE: I remember—

FRANCES: No—

MIKIE: —the way you looked—

FRANCES: —you're crazy—

MIKIE: —in that ugly green jacket—

FRANCES: —No, I said it wasn't me!

MIKIE: Makes you look fatter than you are—

FRANCES: What were you doing there anyway—

MIKIE: I was just watching you.

FRANCES: Some kind of insomniac-pervert—

MIKIE: And I knew what you were doing—

FRANCES: —coming 'round bothering girls in alleys—

MIKIE: —you got dirt still on your hands, underneath your nails.

(*Hiding her hands, she buries them in her coat pockets. She pulls out a lipstick from her pocket*)

FRANCES: Look what I found. (*She laughs*)

MIKIE: Rain doesn't wash the dirt off—

FRANCES (*reading the label*): "Malibu Passion" I forgot I bought it.

(*Looking in the reflection of the window, she puts the lipstick on her washed out face*)

MIKIE: I saw you bending over—

FRANCES: It was only 99 cents at Rossey.

MIKIE: You were digging the dirt out in the alley, with a shovel. You bent over. You were—

(*Suddenly Frances starts to bang her head against the window*)

FRANCES: Aw man—it's raining so fucking hard!

MIKIE: You ·vere burying something.

FRANCES: You can't get the rhythm outta your head. (*She continues to bang her head against the window*) Fuckin' without a tune! —like we're being attacked. Little boys and girls chasing us—little terrorists throwing things at us, running, chasing us, barefoot, cause we forgot to buy them shoes. Or socks. Forgetting everything. (*Screaming to bus driver*) Go faster! This stupid bus is crawling! (*Suddenly weakened, she lies on her back*) The back gets the best bumps, remember?

MIKIE (*nervous*): You got blood on your leg.

FRANCES (*a weak laugh*): It's not coming from my leg.

MIKIE: Maybe you should take an ambulance. (*He quickly stands and walks towards the bus driver*)

FRANCES (*quickly sitting up*): No! No, sit down!

MIKIE: This is stupid. You're bleeding!

FRANCES: Just sit down—

MIKIE: (*To the driver*) She's gonna die—

FRANCES: SHUT UP! (*He stops*) I'm all right—I'm fine.

(*Mikie sits back down in his seat. Mikie, his back to Frances, stares in front of him. Long pause*)

MIKIE (*keeps looking forward*): They're just a mass of flesh anyway.

FRANCES: What?

MIKIE: Babies. You know. Just a mass of flesh. That's all they are—with one hole to scream outta and the other to take a dump.

(*She laughs*)

FRANCES: Yeah, the way they scream and cry—

MIKIE: —and the way they smell like shit—

FRANCES: Yeah—and— and the way they're just there to make you feel bad, when they come out, sometimes, they come out already like a rubber doll and you have to move their feet and arms to pretend . . . they're moving. Already like you did something wrong before you can hold it or comfort it, already gone, like a doll. Before you can give her anything. (*Pause. Mikie turns his head and looks at Frances, who quickly averts her eyes, and stares out the window*) Look, eh? The sun's coming up. Starting to.

MIKIE: You can wait forever for something to happen.

FRANCES: The early morning now—it's the coldest time of the day—

MIKIE: Montreal gets more snow than Moscow. (*Pause. Mikie stands with jacket*)

FRANCES: What are you doing?

MIKIE: It's not too clean.

FRANCES: No, I already have one. (*Pause*) You could sit here if you want. I don't care.

(*Faint, slow ring of four church bells*)

MIKIE: Church bells all over this city.

FRANCES: What time did it say?

MIKIE: Four.

FRANCES: It's been two hours.

(*Pause*)

MIKIE: I used to hate the sound of them. Early in the morning like this? Reminding you, you missed again.

(*Beat*)

FRANCES: It's Catholic—you Catholic?

MIKIE: This whole city is.

FRANCES: You look tired.

MIKIE: No. I'm fine.

FRANCES: You look sleepy.

MIKIE: Just cause I told you—

FRANCES: You could lie down, if you want.

MIKIE: What?

FRANCES: You don't have to sleep.

MIKIE: No.

FRANCES: You can just rest. Your feet up there. (*He puts his feet up and his head on her lap. Long sound of rain as he falls asleep*) No, you don't want to miss anything. (*She looks outside*) That was my stop. (*Mikie is* *asleep*) There's the hospital right there. (*She points to the passing hospital*) Does look like a castle, sort of. (*Beat*) Maybe from the outside. (*Beat*) All lit up like that.

(*She touches his head. Lights down*)

INTERVIEW WITH MADELYN KENT, author of Crawl

Tell us something about your introduction to theater.

I grew up dancing, and then I was in theater programs in public school that let me not go to class because I had to rehearse. One year, my solo was George Benson's "On Broadway." I'd skip out of class and rehearse it a lot. I got to wear a glittery top hat.

What first prompted you to write plays?

When I was in college, there was a one-act festival, and I noticed there were no women writers ever produced in it (although there was one woman who performed a solo on her vagina). So I wrote a play and it was accepted. It was about an eleven-year-old girl who fantasized about seducing and killing Hitler.

What do you think about the state of theater in the U.S. today?

My favorite theater is outside of the U.S.: Robert LePage, from Quebec, for example. I think that the nature of theater in the U.S. is determined by a sense of struggle and self-sacrifice in the content—and in the process of putting on plays—that has been romanticized. That is, a reaction to the difficulty of making theater in America gets made into an aesthetic. It's not necessarily fruitful to the development of exciting work. It just further marginalizes theater and the emotion in theater.

What were you aiming to do with *Crawl*?

I was really connected to the emotion of the characters and the sense of loss they feel. I was just pouring that on the page. Usually I have some intellectual constructions that pull me away from the emotion, but this time I just let it all onto the page.

What are the inspirations for your writing?

Writing *Crawl*, I was in Len Jenkins' class at NYU. He was talking about feeds for playwriting, and he said think of people that you remember from your past. I thought of this woman on a bus in Montreal eight years earlier. I saw her, and I had this urge to follow her. She was the starting point for Frances. Usually, I'm inspired by things that are going on for me personally, which are transformed and either well-disguised or poorly disguised, much to the embarrassment of those close to me.

Is there any advice you would give to aspiring playwrights?

Write from the inside out. In the beginning, it's very seductive to follow formulas or ways of doing things you learn from a teacher. But I wish someone had told me just to write, and trust my intuition, rather than to think about structure.

Voices Within Conflicted Families

Frank: How's my boy gonna be a "handmaiden"?!?
Gus: It's like how you say "fireman," Frank, even if it's a girl . . .
—Henry Kandel, *Gazelle*

Do you ask questions over and over again? Do you forget names or recent events? Do you become lost in familiar places?
—Neena Beber, *Clock*

CONFESSIONS, BEDSIDE
by Jason T. Garrett

Thursday, early afternoon. Bart, 34, sits in the chair alongside his hospital bed. In addition to a variety of tubes, bells and whistles attached to him, his leg is in a cast. He has a moveable IV that he has rolled beside him so that he can sit in the chair. Jon, 29, enters and jumps into Bart's bed.

JON: Quick: what's the meaning of life?

BART (*doesn't look up from his magazine*)**:** Bedsores.

JON: Optimist.

BART: The meaning of life is standing in the cash-only, nine-items-or-less line for fifteen minutes with your single eight-pack of Aunt Jemima low-fat waffles while the Von Trapps in front of you try to pay for their forty-three items with an out-of-country check. Oh, and creating web sites. Seems like the most Bohemian you can be anymore is to not have an e-mail address.

JON: Umm, memo to the last decade: bohemians have e-mail addresses.

BART: Figures. What else do they have to do besides *not* shop for deodorant? Somehow the fifties must've been easier.

JON: Getting thrown in jail for being black, that kinda thing.

BART: I don't mean the *real* fifties. I mean the *Happy Days* fifties.

JON: Ten bucks says Joanie and Jenny Piccolo did the nasty.

BART: Jenny Piccolo. The only flute *Joanie* ever played. I had a nightmare the other day that involved Potsie, Mary Kate and Ashley, and something about a runaway elephant.

JON: Did you totally pop a Mentos before the wackiness ensued?

BART: Gets worse: Don Knotts did a cameo in the shower scene.

JON: Eww. (*Pause*) You're much too sexy for this partially private environment.

BART: *Death Be Not Proud.*

JOHN: Bart . . .

BART: Inertia is *so* overdone.

JON: You're *so* full of shit.

BART: Correction: I am so *not* full of shit. (*Sings*) "The Demon Butthole of Fleet Street."

JON: S'kind of like having a friend with a baby: every conversation involves excrement.

BART: Please, if I were punctuation, I'd be a colon.

JON: But you're a confirmed top, which'd make you only a *semi*colon.

BART: Or perhaps parenthetical. The only thing that makes it tolerable is Mr. Burly Nurse.

JON: The one with the depilatory issues?

BART: "I shave your back, you shave mine."

JON: Lemme know if your HMO stops covering enemas. Then we could all take turns *slapping* the shit outta you.

BART: You wish. (*Pause*) Truth?

JON: Sure.

BART: When I'm butt-up and in the purgative throes of that delightful process known as "evacuation," it's like . . . it's like my entire body is this big, sinking ship, and my body fluids are the . . . they're the rats trying to get off the ship while the getting's good. Like even my waste would rather take its chances on the outside knowing what the odds are on the inside.

JON: Does that qualify as dementia?

BART: You wish I were in dementia: then you *would* have a big wienie.

JON: Do tell: am I blonde or brunette?

BART: In dementia? Brunette on the outside, blonde on the inside.

JON: So my insides have more fun.

BART: No: more people have fun inside you.

JON: What are you in dementia?

BART: Not what: who. Diana Ross. Before the early eighties world tour. After that there were only tragic SuperBowl extravaganzas and having enough skin removed to create a twin sister.

JON: "Breasts by Dow, skin by DuPont." Who really?

BART: Not now.

JON: C'mon.

BART: I said not now.

(*Jon reaches into his pocket, gets something, throws it to Bart*)

JON: Presents.

BART: Ohmigod: You are the Master of the Stealth Twinkie.

JON: Don't forget: it's chock-full of Twinkie goodness.

BART: Didja bring it?

JON: Yeah.

BART: Whadja think?

JON: Like, "friends what did I think" or what did I think?

BART: I'd prefer deception.

(*Jon removes papers from a pocket*)

JON: "It will be a heartfelt occasion crafted from equal parts of whimsy and sentiment."

BART: Gimme the nonfriends version.

JON: I am *not* orchestrating a 21-snap salute for you. It will not happen.

BART: That's the *pièce de résistance.*

JON: I'm also a little concerned about this champagne waterfall you want built from a bedpan and colostomy bags. I think we need to get you out. You've got too much time to think.

BART: It's called running in place, Jon. I don't have the benefit of doing the real thing anymore, so I run in place. Never mind. I'll get Allyn to do it.

JON: At what point did I become the enemy?

BART: Here's a clue: this service isn't about you.

JON: So this monstrosity is about you?

BART: Consider it my little send-up to mortality.

JON: So what? You want everybody to feel your pain? Is that it? 'Cause you know what? That's rich. That's just fucking rich. Of course no one's felt it until now but you, so the experience should be refreshing for all of us.

BART: Tell you what: why don't you go home to your unlimited diet and your day-runner that has wacky plans on it three months from now, and think about what a privilege it is to have those plans and to have a motto like "Live Long and Prosper" instead of "*Carpe Diem*." I am so fucking tired of seizing the fucking day.

JON: No one expects you to know how to die, Bart, so don't expect us to know how to let you go.

BART (*re: the letter*): I'm showing you how to let me go.

JON: No, you're showing us you can still hate."

BART: I burn so many calories walking a mile in your flip-flops. Understanding your grief. It's like a step aerobics class every time somebody comes through that door. (*Pause*) When I used to be able to walk, I sort of fantasized about someone coming up to me on the street and telling me that, at the end of the block, I'd meet my destruction. And, for me, it wasn't a question of whether I'd stop, but whether I could even make myself stop. Now, most days I think I'd rather off myself with bleach and detergent. Except that, if there was an autopsy, people might think I died wanting to be a washing machine.

JON: D'ya think that's why you broke your leg? So you couldn't get to the end of the block?

BART: No, Jon. I broke my leg because getting smothered to death in a big puppy pile isn't in my cards.

JON: I wish that, instead of your destruction, you'd picture all of us there at the end of the block. Everybody there to . . . hold you and find you and tell you you're okay. We could even bring our laundry.

BART: Fucker.

JON: I think falling's good for you. It reminds you of where you come from. It reconnects you to the earth.

BART: You're so Darwin. Please tell me you haven't joined some consciousness-grazing group.

JON: I remain a skeptic.

BART: Thank God. I couldn't deal with being dragged to productions of

Yer Booty's Too Wide to Be Slapped on by Jesus. My kingdom for an agnostic black musical. (*Pause*) Would you call the nurse? I'm feeling less than luscious, and I'm much more telegenic on the other side of a Seconal.

JON (*buzzes the buzzer thing*): Maybe I should get her to bring some fat-reduction lotion too. If there's a thin person inside of me, it's only cause I ate him.

BART: You're not large.

JON: Hyah. Today at the gym I was voted "Person Most Likely to Eat a Gondola of Hostess Fruit Pies."

BART: Jon, I lose roughly three pounds a day through any combination of my orifices, and I'd give anything to have my love handles back.

JON: So is there anything I *can* talk about?

BART: Are you seeing anyone?

JON: Why do you do this? Do you have any idea how unfair it is for you to hate me for small talking and then hate me for being real? What do you want? Tell me.

BART: Tell me we've moved on from Michael Greenburg? Dingoes *should've* eaten that baby.

JON: Bart, what are you scared of?

BART: Direct lighting.

JON: What are you scared of?

BART: Don't do this.

JON: Tell me!

BART: I don't know.

JON: Tell me, Bart. Tell me what you're scared of!

BART: Succeeding, Jon! (*Pause*) I'm scared of succeeding.

JON: At dying?

BART: At chasing you away.

JON (*pause*): Bart, be scared that Disney's on ice. Be scared that we used to sing "99 Red Balloons" in its original German. Be scared that they actually made a movie that brought the Flintstones and the Jetsons together. But don't be scared I'll ever go away.

BART: Yeah?

JON: Yeah.

BART: Sometimes I'm just . . .

JON: I know. It's okay. Being scared is okay. But we're scared *together*.

BART: I've always been more of a Do-It-Yourselfer.

JON: Not anymore.

(*Bart takes the memorial service instructions from Jon and puts them away*)

BART (*Smiles. Pause*): Split a Twinkie?

JON: Yeah.

BART: So what does Michael do?

JON: Management. He's the Head Assistant Key Holder at Baby Gap.

BART: It's good to pace yourself.

(*Lights fade*)

INTERVIEW WITH JASON T. GARRETT, *author of* Confessions, Bedside

Tell us something about your introduction to theater.

I was in the second grade and I was tapped to be in the musical *The Electric Sunshine Man*, which was the story of Thomas Edison. The best part was getting to change costume and sing, and pointing out people we knew onstage while we were supposed to be in character. It was also my introduction to special effects. We had a strobe light on stage, which rocked.

What first prompted you to write plays?

I wrote a novel on the bus each morning in third grade: *The Haunted House of Madison Creek Road*. It was very scary. Everyone on the bus would listen to it, and it was the first time I thought about an audience.

When I was an undergraduate in 1991 I wrote the only full-length I ever did—an office comedy called *The Desktop Ballet*. All my professors who read it said, "I think we all get to the point where we feel we have a play in us, and we write it, and then we just let it go." So I didn't write for several years, but in 1993 I wrote *Umbrella Dancing*, a one act about four twenty-somethings coming of age. It played to sold out houses in Tennessee, and I felt great. It didn't need to be in New York, or hip, or anything; and the fact that it was so strongly accepted pushed me into playwriting again.

What do you think the state of theater is in the U.S. today?

I value places like Soho Rep and Expanded Arts because elsewhere it's death by readings and workshops. There's not a lot of risk-taking, because everyone's shooting for the same idealized subscriber base. These days, only big names are being done at a lot of places. Even in the smallest venues there's a demand for name recognition. Regionally, theater is really getting milquetoast. It's *Best Little Whorehouse in Texas*, part two, Electric Boogaloo.

What were you aiming to do with *Confessions, Bedside*?

Whenever I write a short play I write with a specific technical exercise in mind. For *Confessions, Bedside* I wanted to see if I could get two people who were clearly old friends to a moment of honesty that they'd never had with each other before. Their relationship has to move to the next point or it has to fail utterly. Could I do that in ten pages?

What are the biggest influences on your writing?

J.B. Priestly, Christopher Marlowe, Edward Albee, and Peter Schaeffer. These writers take me to a moment of truth without quotes around it. Their writing negates an intellectual connection because it resonates in your gut. It's flown over your brain and into your body.

Is there any advice you would give to aspiring playwrights?

"Write what you know" does not mean, "Write what you really know." It means, "Write what you know to be emotionally true."

GAZELLE   *by Henry Kandel*

Gus, coach of the little league team, is sitting on the bench tying David's shoes—David is fidgeting with his mitt. Frank, David's father, sits nearby on the bench, forearms resting on thighs. All three are wearing baseball caps.

There are low outdoor game sounds throughout.

GUS: And remember, you're going to play the lefty batters deeper in right field.

FRANK: Pick your head up, David. Listen to what Coach Gus is telling you.

(David stops fidgeting with his glove and looks at Gus)

GUS: See, kiddo? Your dad's as nervous as you are. (*All laugh*) But you're going to be fine out there. Let me see your glove. (*David hands over his glove*) Looks good. Play 'em just like you did in scrimmage. Okay. (*Hunching over David's shoes*) Nice and tight? Good. (*To Frank*) David's a runner. (*To David*) Going to cover the whole field today? (*David nods and smiles*) That's right you are. Going to be like a gazelle. (*Gus gives David an encouraging pat; David runs offstage. Gus and Frank are both sitting on the bench, facing out as they watch the game begin. Long beat*) Female gazelle.

(Beat)

FRANK: What?

GUS: Faster than the male of the species.

(Beat)

FRANK: Yeah?

GUS: Much.

(*Beat*)

FRANK: Yeah, but I don't think . . .

GUS: And a better team player if you really think about it. You know, male's off competing with other males; she's getting down to business.

FRANK (*shaking his head*): I don't know what you're talking about, Gus.

GUS: I'm telling you, Frank. I've never seen more of a female gazelle than in that kid of yours.

FRANK: But . . .

GUS: And David's a born leader.

(*Beat*)

FRANK (*relaxing*): You think?

GUS: No doubt about it. Other kids on the team—they just rally around him. He's got a gift.

FRANK (*smiling*): Yeah?

GUS: True leader. (*Long beat*) Queen bee.

(*Beat*)

FRANK: Huh?!?

GUS: Best damn field marshal in the world, if you really think about it.

FRANK: Wait . . .

GUS: Has to keep the drones on the move.

FRANK: Look here . . .

GUS: You know, they'll die for the queen. They'll die for her.

FRANK: David is not . . . look. David is a damn good ballplayer.

GUS: No argument there.

(*Beat*)

FRANK: For his age, a *damn* good ballplayer.

GUS: The best I've got. The best I've got. No telling how good that kid's going to be. (*Frank relaxes a little. Long beat*) If he keeps growing like a pansy.

(*Beat*)

FRANK: What?!?

GUS: Fastest growing wildflower there is.

FRANK: Yeah, but my kid's . . .

GUS: Shoots up like nothing.

FRANK: Gus . . .

GUS: No matter how bad the soil.

FRANK: Now look here . . .

GUS: Yep. Never seen more of a pansy than that kid.

FRANK: Don't call my kid a pansy, okay?

GUS: I was giving David a compliment, Frank.

FRANK: Just don't call my kid a pansy.

GUS: I wasn't trying to . . .

FRANK: Just don't.

GUS: Jeez.

FRANK: He's not a queen or anything either.

GUS: But Frank . . .

FRANK: Okay?

GUS: But if you really think about it . . .

FRANK: Okay?!?

(*Beat*)

GUS: Look at David on the on-deck circle . . . Sweetest swing I've seen in all the years I've been here.

FRANK: Really . . . ?

GUS: The perfect arc.

FRANK: Ever . . . ?

GUS: Almost perfect enough to summon the Goddess.

FRANK (*standing up*): Allright, Gus . . . !

(*Boom! Flickering lights. The Goddess Ishtar appears, wearing golden armor with cone-shaped boobs*)

FRANK: Holy shit!

GUS: Ishtar!

ISHTAR: What is this perfect arc I see here in this land and century?

FRANK: Holy . . . !

GUS (*bowing down*): Merciful Goddess, he is my clean-up hitter, a boy called David.

ISHTAR: "David."

FRANK: W . . . wait a second here . . . who the hell are you?!?

ISHTAR: I am Ishtar, Goddess of War and Fertility.

FRANK: Huh . . .

GUS: She's extended her realm to include war games.

ISHTAR: Coach Gus speaks true.

FRANK: But this is baseball!

GUS: The Mayans played a similar game with human heads.

ISHTAR: The boy shall be my handmaiden.

FRANK: Now you hold on . . . !

GUS: It's a great honor, Frank.

FRANK: How's my boy gonna be a "maiden"?!?

GUS: It's like how you say "fireman," Frank, even if it's a girl . . .

FRANK: No way!

GUS: Joe DiMaggio was one, Frank.

FRANK: Joe . . . ?

ISHTAR: He served me well. As did Charlemagne and Attila the Hun. And the Babe of Ruth.

GUS: Best damn handmaiden of 'em all.

FRANK: Now let me tell you something, whoever you are . . . !

(*Ishtar gestures and Frank freezes. He can still move his eyes and grunt*)

GUS: I should have warned you, the Goddess don't like to be trifled with.

ISHTAR: I have been around for too many centuries . . .

(*A loud "crack" is heard and sounds of a cheering crowd. Ishtar and Gus watch the flight of the ball*)

GUS: Wow, what a shot!

ISHTAR: Come to me, boy.

(*David trots onstage, exuberant, out of breath*)

DAVID: What'd you think of that, Dad? (*Beat. Frank grunts. Ishtar gestures at him and he refreezes in a position with his thumb up and a big grin stuck on his face. He grunts again*)

DAVID: Thanks, Dad.

GUS: David, I'd like you to meet Ishtar.

DAVID: The Goddess of War and Fertility!

GUS: Yes.

DAVID: And, by extension, war games!

GUS: That's right.

DAVID: I sacrificed a caterpillar to you in second grade!

ISHTAR: I remember, David. Though I did not know then that you would become a great warrior.

DAVID: Gee, thanks!

GUS: Ishtar would like you to be her handmaiden, David.

DAVID: Cool! What do I gotta do?

ISHTAR: You need to sign this contract. In blood, of course.

(*She takes out an enormous scroll. Frank grunts loudly in protest*)

GUS: It's a great honor, David.

ISHTAR: You get a thousand home runs, each far longer than the one you just hit, many of them in the so-called Major Leagues. I get your first World Series ring and a lamb every other solstice.

DAVID: Cool! (*He signs it*)

ISHTAR: I'll also need the signature of the coach.

(*Frank grunts in protest*)

GUS: Sure. (*He signs*) Whoop, that's three outs. Okay, kid, show the Goddess how you play the field!

DAVID: You bet! (*He runs off*)

ISHTAR: Ah, I see another perfect arc, this one in Persia. I must go.

GUS: One small favor, Goddess?

ISHTAR: Speak, Coach Gus.

GUS: The father of the handmaiden.

ISHTAR: Oh, yes . . .

(*She gestures at Frank, unfreezing him, and disappears with a "boom!" and a flickering of lights*)

FRANK (*slumping on the bench*): How . . . what . . . I—

GUS: It's okay, Frank.

FRANK: Did . . . you . . . see . . . ?

GUS: David's homer? A beauty.

FRANK: I . . . I . . .

GUS It's okay, Frank. (*Taking Frank's head on his shoulder*) You need a good cry.

(*Frank weeps on Gus's shoulder. Fade to black.*)

INTERVIEW WITH HENRY KANDEL,
author of Gazelle

What first prompted you to write plays?

In Off Off Campus, the University of Chicago improv group, we had three weeks to put on a show—writing, directing, producing. So, deadlines got me writing. We had to just churn out skits.

Tell us something about your introduction to theater.

I was really into Fred Astaire and Ginger Rogers when I was five. I took dance classes and I would totally ham it up. We had this final performance for all the parents and I mimed a cane and a top hat and pretended to tap dance. I wound up quitting though, because I was the only boy in the class, with seventeen girls. The message was so clear to me that dancing is not for boys. But I broke through that. Now I hit the dance floor, and I hit it good.

How would you characterize your own writing?

For me, having a relatively decent day job [teaching high-school physics] means that I'm not trying to write the next great American screenplay. Improv defines my writing—not sketch comedy, but long-form improv that is character-based. I'm writing more and more scripts that don't include dialogue, and even when I do write dialogue, the things that happen are very much like the things that happen in improv.

What were you aiming to do with *Gazelle*?

I was aiming to wrestle with past demons. I played little league, and I'm taking a jab at the kind of machismo that surrounded me growing up on Long Island. All of my plays are exorcisms.

Where do you situate your work in relation to mainstream American culture?

I expect the mainstream American to have no appreciation whatsoever for what I do. And I hope it remains this way.

Given the minimal financial rewards for writing for the stage, why do you do it?

Catharsis. It saves me therapy bills.

DINNER   *by Lucy Thurber*

A posh dining room. Bay windows back centerstage. Mother Milford paces waiting for her son. Sonny Milford enters stage left.

MOTHER: You're late.

SONNY: Yes I know.

MOTHER: Where have you been?

SONNY: The office.

(*A wailing is heard offstage. Aunt Mitilda runs by outside the windows naked. Sonny and Mother watch her pass. Short pause*)

MOTHER: Sit down with me please. (*They both sit*) Lilia called me today.

SONNY: She's a bitch.

MOTHER: Yes dear. But she called, and I understand . . .

SONNY: I wouldn't believe a word she tells you, all she wants is our money. (*Outside the windows Aunt Mitilda runs by naked followed by Grandfather Peter. He is wearing a safari hat and carrying a big net*) You do know company is coming. What's for dinner? Cook! Cook! (*Betty comes in dressed in cook clothes*) What's for dinner Cook?

BETTY: Leg of lamb sir.

SONNY: Leg of lamb, you lousy whore?! We had leg of lamb two days ago! (*He grabs her and forces her over the table and lifts up her skirt and starts raping her*)

MOTHER: She says she's pregnant, son. She says she's carrying your child.

SONNY: Umm, ummm—

BETTY: Are you done yet sir? The lamb, it's burning.

SONNY: Umm, ummm—

MOTHER: A child of yours. A new Milford. I want that child Sonny. The little pattering feet. You must get married.

BETTY: Sir could you please hurry . . .

SONNY: I'm trying, I'm trying, I can't seem to . . .

MOTHER: The situation itself is embarrassing. Not finding out from you . . . I'm not sure what to say Sonny . . . I'm mortified . . .

BETTY: Oh for God's sake Sonny! (*She bucks, dislodging him. She swishes down her skirts*) Really Sonny, so much for the ruling class, I thought you'd be masterful. You're boring, in out, in out same as any one! I'm terribly disappointed! (*She storms off*)

SONNY: What a woman! I had no idea! Such passion and fire! Such movement . . . oh Cook . . . Cook . . .

MOTHER: Sonny, please zip up your pants when I'm speaking to you!

(*Grandfather enters with naked Aunt Mitilda in his net*)

GRANDFATHER: Hello, hello . . . look what I caught. The white man in the jungle . . . a beautiful naked beast . . . lovely, lovely . . .

(*The doorbell rings*)

MOTHER: That will be Mitty and her guest.

SONNY: My God! (*He zips up his fly*) My sister! My sister is home!

MOTHER: A guest, a friend from school . . .

(*They all mutter "guest, guest"*)

AUNT MITILDA: I must dress. My goodness, a guest.

GRANDFATHER: I must change. My goodness, a guest.

SONNY: My sister! My beautiful sister!

MOTHER (*ringing a bell*): Prepare for dinner!

(*End of scene*)

Scene Two

The grand hallway. Mitty and Sarah enter.

MITTY: What do you see? Describe it to me.

SARAH: A hallway, marble. A grand staircase.

MITTY: And how does that make you feel?

SARAH: Small.

MITTY: Interesting. Small how?

SARAH: Small in a tiny way.

MITTY: I see. I see. And what do you smell?

SARAH: You.

MITTY: I smell like marble and stair?

SARAH: Like ice.

MITTY: I shall kiss you for that. (*She kisses Sarah*)

SARAH: Thank you.

MITTY: Open your coat. (*Sarah opens her coat. She is wearing a woman's tailored suit*) My clothes look good on you Sarah. (*She cups Sarah's breast*) Does that excite you?

SARAH: It frightens me.

MITTY: Good, fear is exciting. (*Running her hands down Sarah's neck to her breasts*) And I frighten you.

SARAH: Always.

MITTY: My kisses?

SARAH: Yes.

MITTY: My hair?

SARAH: Yes. I have no idea how you keep it so straight. Even in the morning it is straight.

MITTY: And my teeth?

SARAH: So white.

MITTY: I'm so glad you've come. We'll have a wonderful night.

(*Betty enters dressed as a maid*)

BETTY: I'm sorry I kept you waiting Miss. We mustn't tell your Mom . . .

MITTY: Fucking in the kitchen again? You lead such an interesting life. I've always admired your ability to be free with your body. I live under such constraints.

(*Mitty takes off her coat and dangles it. She drops it. Betty lunges, catching it before it hits the ground*)

SARAH (*handing Betty her coat*): Something in the way you move reminds me of my Ma.

BETTY: I ain't your Ma. I've kept track of all my children.

SARAH: No. But you have her hair.

BETTY: Don't insult me.

SARAH: I'm not. I recognize you.

BETTY: It's like that, is it?

SARAH: It is.

BETTY: Well aren't you special? (*Whispering to Sarah*) I hope she's better than her brother. I've found him a terrible disappointment. (*Out loud*) They're having lamb.

(*Betty exits with the coats*)

MOTHER (*offstage*): Darling! Darling Mitty is that you!? Is that my baby girl?!

(*Mitty smiles and tries to reach under Sarah's skirt. Sarah jumps away*)

MITTY: I'm here Mother. I brought my friend. Don't be frightened Sarah, and don't get shy on me either. That's not what you're here for. (*She reaches for her again*) Come quickly now, they'll be on us any second.

(*Sarah steps back again. Sonny enters*)

SONNY: Well Mitty, I've missed you terribly these last few months. I've been reduced to fucking lots of girls I care nothing about. Abusing their feelings, sometimes hurting them physically, and it's all your fault. I'm more lonely than you could know, without you here to look after me.

MITTY: Hello Sonny.

(*Mother enters. Crossing to Mitty*)

MOTHER: Darling, kiss, kiss.

MITTY: Hello Mother.

MOTHER: And who is your little friend?

MITTY: This is Sarah. She's on scholarship.

MOTHER: Really? How charming. You do bring home the most exciting people, Mitty. Sarah, welcome, welcome. I've never met someone on scholarship before. You must tell us all about it.

SARAH: Yes . . . well . . . I—

MOTHER: And polite. How interesting. Sarah, is that a Jewish name? We're Episcopalian.

MITTY: Jesus Mother, poor people aren't religious. They're superstitious. Everyone knows that.

MOTHER: You're right. How embarrassing. I hope I haven't offended you, Sarah.

SARAH: I'm Catholic.

MOTHER: Of course you are. How cute.

SONNY (*who has been staring forlornly at Mitty this whole time*)**:** My God, you look beautiful tonight, Mitty.

MITTY: Yes Sonny, of course I do. I'm a very beautiful young woman. I've learned not to be afraid of my beauty or try to hide it.

SONNY: And so confident and secure! How I admire you.

MOTHER: It's wonderful to see siblings so close. Isn't it? Tell me Sarah, do you have any brothers or sisters?

SARAH: I . . .

MOTHER: Right! Let's all retire to the study. Drinks and hors d'oeuvres, everyone!

(*End of scene*)

Scene Three

The study. Grandfather and Sonny sit in chairs. Mother and Aunt Mitilda sit on a couch. The Maid stands by with a drink tray. Sarah and Mitty wander around the room.

SONNY (*holding out his glass*): More martini.

(*Betty rushes, pouring into his glass*)

GRANDFATHER: In the war . . .

MOTHER: Jesus was a Jew . . .

AUNT MITILDA: Yes.

MOTHER: A Jew, but we're Christians.

AUNT MITILDA: Yes.

GRANDFATHER: In the war, men were men.

SARAH (*to Mitty*): You're beautiful in the firelight. I'm so grateful to you for liking me.

GRANDFATHER: In the war . . .

MOTHER: But Jesus was a Jew.

AUNT MITILDA: Yes.

MOTHER: He cleaned the peddlers out of the Church.

AUNT MITILDA: Yes.

MOTHER: Clearing the way for Christianity.

GRANDFATHER: In the war we kicked some Nazi ass. Never should of left those women alone. Working in factories, fucking the cripples, while good men lost their cocks.

SONNY (*holding up his glass*): Maid.

(*Betty quickly refills his glass*)

SARAH: What's this?

MITTY: A painting. Shall I explain it to you?

SARAH: Please.

MITTY: Fundamentally, it's man's relation to nature. Man is small. Nature is big.

(*Sonny raises his glass. Betty hurries to fill it*)

AUNT MITILDA: I've lost my hat. My hat with the birds.

MOTHER: One thing I can say about birds. They sure do fly about.

AUNT MITILDA: Still, I've lost my hat. I noticed it the other day. (*She stares meaningfully at Betty*) Do you suppose? I mean she probably just came from prison.

(*Sony raises his glass. Betty hurries to fill it*)

SARAH: What's this?

MITTY (*Mitty takes Sarah's hand and puts it on her breast*): My breast under crushed velvet.

SARAH: How could anything be this beautiful. I think I might faint.

BETTY (*ringing a little bell on the drink tray*): Dinner is served.

(*End of scene*)

Scene Four

They all sit around the dining room table.

SONNY: In Switzerland, Sarah, that's where I went to school.

SARAH (*whispering to Mitty*): They seem to like me.

SONNY: In Switzerland, where I was taught good posture . . .

MOTHER: I love the fall. Don't you just love the fall, Sarah?

SARAH (*whispering to Mitty*): This is going well. Much better than I expected.

MOTHER: The fall is when I met your father, kids.

SONNY: Women in black, walking around with large sticks. They'd crack you in the ribs if you weren't at a 90 degree angle. That's why I'm so beautiful today.

MOTHER: Your father was so handsome in his football jacket. Muscular like a young bull and so prized. Prized by us all. The perfect example of what a man should be.

SONNY: Not like women today. Walking down the streets, looking exactly like apes. That's what they are. Apes. No class, no dignity.

MOTHER: And I felt passion. Passion, deep, deep inside. The kind of passion only a good girl can feel.

GRANDFATHER: I can't remember, Sarah, but it seems I was with IBM then; South America division. Good those Latins know how to screw.

AUNT MITILDA: Please pass the peas.

SONNY: I'm going to kill myself Mitty. Don't think I won't. Right here at the table with this butter knife. I'm going to bleed to death right in front of you. What do you think about that?

GRANDFATHER: And the parties . . .

AUNT MITILDA: Yes, the parties . . .

MOTHER: The parties we used to have. Not like today.

AUNT MITILDA: Nothing like today.

GRANDFATHER: And how we'd dance.

SONNY: It's tragic. The love I feel is tragic. Never to have you the way I should. You're mine by birth. You're mine by blood. How many of those little college punks do you let fiddle you in the dark, Mitty?

MITTY:　I've been learning a lot at college, Sonny. No one is in charge of a woman's passion. It is my obligation. My right. My duty to explore my sexuality before I marry. I'm no different than you Sonny. I'm claiming my power in a male-dominated world. Where the rights of woman have been shat upon. I'm not scared anymore Sonny, I've been taking a feminist theory class. It's opened my eyes to a lot of things. A lot of awful things. I'm setting myself free, Sonny. So when I marry and settle down, I'll be the right kind of woman.

SONNY:　God I respect you!

GRANDFATHER:　And my God, Jews and blacks in the Country Club. Now don't get me wrong. I've got nothing against the odd charity case, right Sarah? But we have to keep people in their places. There's a God given order, an order that must be contained.

AUNT MITILDA:　The meat is overdone. You really should fire that Cook, Sister.

MOTHER:　Yes, but she makes the most wonderful desserts. I don't think I could live without her pecan pie. Do you like pecan pie Sarah? Oh that's right, you've probably never had it before? Well, tonight's a big treat.

SARAH:　I'm not feeling too well.

MOTHER:　It's all the rich food. I'm sure you're not used to it.

AUNT MITILDA:　Eat it slowly. That's my advice. But who listens to me.

MOTHER:　You must save room for dessert, Sarah. Promise me. It would be such a shame if you didn't try everything.

AUNT MITILDA:　At least she doesn't have to worry about watching her weight.

MOTHER:　No. But her complexion with all that welfare food. It's all starch. You must try some protein dear.

GRANDFATHER: Goddamn FDR and all that welfare shit. Makes me ashamed to live in this country. Nothing to believe in any more. The fucken cripples and fags got their hands in everything. We need a purge, a goddamn cleansing.

SARAH: I'm not feeling too well, Mitty. I'm really not. I want to go home.

MOTHER (*clapping her hands*): Oh! I have a marvelous idea. Mitty, why not let Sarah go through the Goodwill clothes? (*To Sarah*) It would be so much nicer for them to go to someone we know.

SARAH (*standing*): I'm sorry . . . I have to . . . I'm really not feeling well at all. If I could just have my coat. I can walk to the train station from here.

MOTHER: Oh how delightful Mitty, she wants to walk.

MITTY: Sit down Sarah, you're embarrassing me.

SARAH: I'm sorry . . . I . . .

MOTHER: No need to apologize.

AUNT MITILDA: No, no . . .

GRANDFATHER: No need.

SONNY: We're out of the goddamn wine. How many times do you have to tell her mother . . .

(*Betty enters and begins clearing the plates*)

SONNY (*taking the empty wine bottle and waving it at her*): Hello wine . . .

SARAH: Mom?

BETTY: Your Mom's not here, love. You're all alone.

SARAH: I really don't feel so well Mom.

BETTY: That's only to be expected. Don't worry. You'll get used to it.

You'll forget. It's the nature of things, my love. You'll find it hard to remember anything. It's nothing to worry about, it happens to everyone. And isn't it wonderful to be rich? Of course it is. Look around you. Your wildest dreams have come true. Don't be afraid of sleepy mediocrity. That's my advice to you. (*Betty exits*)

MOTHER: And now it's time for dessert. And a toast. (*They all raise their glasses*) To Sarah, who has courage and smarts. Surviving all the gangs and homelessness. Not succumbing to welfare and pregnancy. To Sarah, who made it out. Here, here. Here, here. (*Etc.*)

(*Lights fade to black*)

INTERVIEW WITH LUCY THURBER, *author of* Dinner

What is your background as a playwright?

I was newly out of college, and I got a job doing electrics at the Eugene O'Neill Playwrights' Conference. There, I met a woman named Kate Robin who was a member of The Playwrights' Collective, and she took me in. I joined the collective, and Eduardo Muchado taught a free class there. I took it for three years, and that was all she wrote.

Tell us something about your introduction to theater.

When I was about seven, this woman my mother knew did summer stock at an amphitheater out in the woods. She was doing *As You Like It*, and she wanted me to be in the play because she thought I looked like I'd be a good actress. I was the only kid. I played a page, and I sang a little song. My love affair with theater began at that point, and I never wanted to do anything else.

What do you think about the state of theater in the U.S. today?

There's not a lot of money, so that makes it difficult for every generation of playwright. You're kind of bucking your head up against the status quo. My generation will eventually be the ones in charge, and then there will be a bunch of younger people saying how we used to be so cutting edge (but now we're not)! The state of American theater is that professional theater is really for the rich, and that's problematic.

Dramatically, what were you aiming to do with *Dinner*?

I'd been reading a lot of Joe Orton. I wanted to write a farce in that vein. But actually, I started with the opening image of a crazy naked aunt running around with her father chasing her with a butterfly net—and from there it took off. I write about class in America, and *Dinner* is a story about the rising lower classes and what happens to them when they try to make it rich.

Who are the biggest inspirations for your writing?

The people I grew up with, because they were all extremely poor. I'm interested in giving a voice to the experiences and people that I've known in my life.

What about playwrights?

I love Chekov. In terms of Americans, I love Tennessee Williams. He's a really dangerous writer, not afraid to get to the very dark places in our society and in ourselves.

Given the minimal financial rewards for writing for the stage, why do you do it?
I'm in love with the stage. There's something about live theater, about being in the audience when the play is good, and the actors are good, and the production is good. There's nothing else like it. . . . It's one of the oldest ways that western society has come together as a community.

Is there any advice you would give to aspiring playwrights?
Worry about your plays. Don't worry about your career. Your only real job is to write your next play. In it, try do deal with whatever it was you were unable to deal with in the play you just finished. Your job is to write, and to try to always write better.

CLOCK   *By Neena Beber*

Characters:

The daughter as she imagines herself Older.

The daughter as she remembers herself Younger.

The Imagined Daughter of someone else.

The Imagined Father of someone else.

A Stranger who cannot remember if he is a father.

The younger daughter and the imagined daughter can be played by the same actress. The imagined father and the stranger can also double.

OLDER: I used to read Dear Abby as a child.
I used to read it and
I'm trying to get this right
it was a green couch
where I'd lie
sprawled across papers (the Sunday news)
on Sundays.
I used to read Dear Abby as a child
I don't know why.

STRANGER: Do you suffer from memory loss?

OLDER: What?

STRANGER: Do you—

OLDER: Are you speaking to me?

STRANGER: —suffer—

OLDER: Doesn't—

STRANGER: What was I asking?

OLDER: —everyone?
        I used to read Dear Abby in childhood.
        It started when I was little.
        It was simple   to read
        and something about it caught my eye.

(*Another scenario:*)

IMAGINED DAUGHTER: I don't want to call her "Auntie" anymore.

IMAGINED FATHER: But she is your Auntie.

IMAGINED DAUGHTER: It's too stupid—Auntie—I don't like saying that.

IMAGINED FATHER: What would you like to call her then?

IMAGINED DAUGHTER: What you call her.

IMAGINED FATHER: I call her tatums and delicious and bobonuts and sweet tits.

IMAGINED DAUGHTER: Oh.

IMAGINED FATHER: You see?

(*They become frozen*)

OLDER: I remember the green couch on which I would read
        Dear Abby
        (Was it Sundays only?).
        Now a certain kind of nostalgia for
        the green couch
        and
        and not just the green couch
        the
        something I am remembering I am trying to . . .

STRANGER: Do you suffer from memory loss?

OLDER: Do I know you?

STRANGER: Do you or do you have a loved one who—

OLDER: What?

STRANGER: —forgets?

OLDER: Do I? Do I know you? Do I?

STRANGER: Do you ask questions over and over again?
Do you forget names or recent events?
Do you become lost in familiar places?

OLDER: That's a trick question, isn't it?

(*The other scenario unfreezes:*)

IMAGINED DAUGHTER: I've thought of what I should call her.

IMAGINED FATHER: Have you?

IMAGINED DAUGHTER: Mrs. Simonson.

IMAGINED FATHER: What are you thinking?

IMAGINED DAUGHTER: Ms.?

IMAGINED FATHER: I must not have taught you well.

IMAGINED DAUGHTER: Erica, then?

IMAGINED FATHER: Nasty.

IMAGINED DAUGHTER: It's her name.

IMAGINED FATHER: She's been a mother to you.

IMAGINED DAUGHTER: I have a mother.

IMAGINED FATHER: You have two.

(*They become frozen*)

OLDER: The couch was green, green like
　　　　　　an olive, green like the skin
　　　　　　of an avocado but soft,
　　　　　　and I lay
　　　　　　on papers
　　　　　　the day's news scattered
　　　　　　while in the next room the TV chattered
　　　　　　with the game my father watched
　　　　　　his one day off;
　　　　　　a loud drone coming from the TV and—

STRANGER: Do you suffer from memory?

OLDER: —and and and my father—

STRANGER: That's what I was asking, right?

OLDER: —my father in the next room—

STRANGER: Do you suffer?

OLDER: —my not watching with him.

STRANGER: Do you feel loss in familiar places?

OLDER: If I could have been a son I would have, I should have tried to be—

STRANGER: Do you have trouble staying home safely?

OLDER: —a son.

(*The other scenario unfreezes:*)

IMAGINED DAUGHTER: Do you love her better than me?

IMAGINED FATHER: Why do you imagine such a question?

IMAGINED DAUGHTER: I don't want to call her Auntie and maybe that's because I imagine such a question.

IMAGINED FATHER: Hmm.

IMAGINED DAUGHTER: Do you love her the way you loved my mother?

IMAGINED FATHER: I never loved your mother.

IMAGINED DAUGHTER: Oh.

(*They remain still but unfrozen*)

OLDER: My father in the next room was younger than I am now
but I thought him old.
He watched the ball game alone on Sundays
because he didn't have a boy.
I was in the next room
on the green couch
the paper on me and under me.
He had already read it but not Dear Abby
I don't think
don't think he would have.

YOUNGER: Sep-a-rate.
It isn't difficult.
The word even suggests
the possibility
contains
a hidden syllable
in the middle.
Someday I shall
Someday I shall
write down words, names, whatever I want.

STRANGER: Do you suffer from memory loss?

YOUNGER: Not that I—

OLDER: Or do you suffer more when you remember?

YOUNGER: —will recall—

STRANGER: What was I asking?

YOUNGER: —this.

(*Older turns to the stranger*)

STRANGER: Do you suffer from memory?
                        Do you suffer from loss?
                        Do you?—

YOUNGER: Dear Abby:

STRANGER: —in familiar places—

YOUNGER: My father is in the next room watching television.

STRANGER: —suffer?

YOUNGER: When I grow to be his age I'll think myself young
                        but now I think him old.
                        When I grow to be his age my father will be . . .

(*The younger looks for where he might be. The older shakes her head. He is gone*)

YOUNGER: I would like to know why I do not
                        walk into the next room
                        and how can I now
                        walk into the next room
                        Dear Abby why do I stay on the green couch
                        reading Dear Abby
                        when my father—

OLDER: Memory:
                        (papers scattered earlier by my father
                        on the green couch
                        where I now lie)

YOUNGER: —when my father—

OLDER: Loss:

YOUNGER: —is in the next room . . .

OLDER: (wanting so much wanting so much my father)

(*Everyone freezes and then is gone. The End*)

INTERVIEW WITH NEENA BEBER, *author of* Clock

What is your professional background as a playwright?
I've been trying to do TV writing to make a living, and playwriting for myself. While I'm doing TV, my plays tend to come out stranger, because naturalistic dialogue sounds like television to me.

What first prompted you to write plays?
A book that really affected me was Mac Wellman's anthology, *Theatre of Wonders*. I became interested initially in that kind of language-based theater.

What were you aiming to do with *Clock*?
Part of it was the formal challenge of the assignment the Summer Camp producers gave me, which was to use a "Dear Abby" column somehow. The "Dear Abby" I chose was right next to a "movie clock," and that was next to an ad for people suffering from memory problems: "Do you have a friend or loved one who has memory loss?" I used that whole newspaper page to make connections. Also, I had recently contributed to a ten-minute play festival in which I had been told to write a metaphysical work, and that inspired me to address issues of time and space overtly.

What are the biggest influences or inspirations for your writing?
Usually, a fragment of language or an image. Martin Epstein, Len Jenkin, Adrienne Kennedy, Murray Mednick, William Alfred, Mac Wellman—they were all important teachers for me. Poetry is a big influence in a certain kind of play. I read Derek Wolcott, Mark Strand, Howard Nemerov.

Given the minimal financial rewards for writing for the stage, why do you do it?
I ask myself this everyday. It's a strange addiction. I like the collaboration that happens, and the rawness, the intimacy, feeling part of an event. I'll always be attracted to small, black box theater work.

Is there any advice you would give to aspiring playwrights?
Find the people you want to work with and be self-producing. Try to direct the way your work is seen, instead of sending it out into the void and hoping someone will do it. You can connect with other people and create places to do your work.

THE FRIENDLY NEIGHBORHOOD
By Michael D. Chung

Thematic Note

Arthur Schopenhauer, in volume one of *The World as Will and Representation*, writes, "this visible world in which we are, a magic effect called into being, an unstable and inconstant illusion without substance, comparable to the optical illusion and the dream, a veil enveloping human consciousness, a something of which it is equally false and equally true to say that it is and it is not." Experience is merely a representation of reality. It is an appearance and illusion. More specifically, experience is a product of interactions between perceiving agent and the world as it truly is, in and of itself, independent of experience. Consequently, knowledge (in the form of absolutes—scientific, philosophical, religious, and moral) derived from experience is itself illusory.

We are impressionist artists. We extract absolutes (secondary illusions) from experience (primary illusions) and allow those absolutes to condition the initial experience until we are no longer living inside appearances and representations of reality, but impressions of appearances and representations (tertiary illusions)

Equation for the Formation of Tertiary Illusions

$AB \times Y = ABY$

AB = primary illusions (experiences or appearances and representations of reality)

Y = secondary illusions (absolutes)

ABY = tertiary illusions (impressions of appearances and representations)

Tertiary illusions thus create a nearly impenetrable mask, disguising the world as it truly is, in and of itself.

Schopenhauer, in volume two of the same work, writes that the world as it truly is, in and of itself, consists of irrational forces in perpetual conflict. The result is brutality, meaninglessness, and suffering. Both the perceiving agent and the world as it truly is, in and of itself, contribute to the formation of tertiary illusions. The latter contributes perpetual conflict, brutality, and so on, while the former contributes secondary illusions—absolutes developed out of the perceiving agent's inability to accept the inevitability of perpetual conflict, brutality, and so on.

(Expanded) Equation for the Formation of Tertiary Illusions

(1) $A \leftarrow B = AB$

A = the world as it truly is, in and of itself (perpetual conflict, brutality, meaninglessness, and suffering). $\leftarrow$ = "is perceived by"

B = perceiving agent

AB = appearances and representations of reality (or the world as it truly is, in and of itself).

(2) $A \rightarrow B \rightarrow Y$

A = the world as it truly is, in and of itself (perpetual conflict, brutality, meaninglessness, and suffering).

$\rightarrow B \rightarrow$ = "inspires in B"

Y = secondary illusions (absolutes)

(3) $AB \times Y = ABY$

AB = primary illusions (appearances and representations of reality)

Y = secondary illusions (absolutes)

ABY = tertiary illusions (impressions of appearances and representations)

The sole constant in these equations is A, or the world as it truly is, in and of itself. Y, and therefore ABY, are of a nebulous nature; absolutes are forever being modified or discarded (and consequently impressions are changing form) to accommodate the relentless thrust of perpetual conflict, brutality, and so on. It is this kaleidoscopic quality of our illusions which causes us to lose faith in them. However, we continue in our absurd struggle to impose meaning on what is essentially meaningless, and take a positive perspective on a state of affairs that is irredeemably evil.

Characters:

Brighella, the Clown

The Circus Ringmaster

Pagliacci, the Clown

Rodrigo, the Clown

A Snare Drummer

Lights up on Pagliacci in the Clown's house.

Flimsy cardboard and paper walls enclose a space so small that a human being could not possibly live here. The walls are painted in bright and happy pastels. Painted windows look out at rolling clouds and a smiley-face sun. A friendly neighbor is painted into another window; dressed in an apron and chef's hat, he barbecues hamburgers on a Weber and waves his spatula in a friendly gesture of "hello." Framed pictures that say "Home Is Where the Heart Is" and "Home Sweet Home" hang from the cardboard walls. Pieces of furniture, also painted in happy pastels, are constructed so as to negate their function—slanted tables, chairs without legs and backs, a clock with no hands. Pagliacci's house suggests a world that is at once benevolent and contradictory, happy and illusory.

A snare drummer, dressed in a powder-blue tuxedo, sits behind a blue-sparkle snare drum and symbol.

The Circus Ringmaster, dressed in a black top hat, a red tuxedo jacket with tails, equestrian trousers and leather boots, enters the house. He is carrying a heavy, bloodstained burlap sack over his shoulder. An applause track plays.

He stamps the mud off his boots and slams the cardboard door shut behind him; the entire house trembles under the impact. A moment later, we hear the sound of a door slamming; the soundman missed his cue. The Circus Ringmaster does a double take at the door. A laugh track plays. The laugh track is played periodically during the course of the play.

Brighella, the Clown enters from offstage. She is wearing an apron that says, "Home Is Where the Heart Is" and carrying a plate with a napkin draped over the top.

BRIGHELLA: Why if it isn't the Circus Ringmaster! Hello, there, Circus Ringmaster!

CIRCUS RINGMASTER: My, my. You're looking mighty pretty these days, Miss Brighella. You smell like shit, but you're looking mighty pretty. Hell, if you weren't a clown, I might just consider courting you away from your hubby!

BRIGHELLA (*giggling*): Oh, stop, you dirty old sonofabitch you! (*A shocked Ringmaster looks at the audience with an expression that seems*

to say, "Did she just say what I think she said?") I smell like shit because
we live in the stables with the livery horses, remember?

CIRCUS RINGMASTER: Ohhhh, that's right. I hope that's not too incon-
venient for you and your family.

(*She presents the plate*)

BRIGHELLA: I just baked a fresh batch of my world famous chocolate
chip cookies. Would you like to be my guinea pig and try one?

CIRCUS RINGMASTER: Why Brighella, the Baking Clown! Don't
mind if I do. (*Brighella snaps the napkin away from the plate, as if she
were performing a magic trick. The plate is empty*) Why Miss Brighella,
that there plate is empty.

BRIGHELLA (*puts her fingers to her lips*): Shhhhh. Since you pay us such
a pitiful salary, I couldn't afford real chocolate chip cookies, so I had to
bake imaginary ones. (*Agreeing to play along, the Circus Ringmaster
gives Brighella an exaggerated wink of the eye. He rolls up his sleeves,
licks his lips in anticipation, and picks up an imaginary cookie. He bites
and chews in exaggerated fashion, pretending to savor every morsel*) Well?
What do you think of my heavenly chocolate chip cookies?

CIRCUS RINGMASTER: These are more delicious than real chocolate
chip cookies, because you can pretend that they were baked in the finest
bakery in Paris. You don't believe me? (*He takes the plate*) Try one and
see for yourself.

(*She rolls up her sleeves*)

BRIGHELLA: Now, I don't usually eat my cooking. After all, we girls
have to watch our weight. But I'll let this one slide. (*She eats in the same
exaggerated fashion*) Mmmm.

CIRCUS RINGMASTER: What did I tell you? Can you taste that rich
milk chocolate?

BRIGHELLA: I think there's a hint of ginger in mine.

(*The Circus Ringmaster puts down his bloody burlap sack with difficulty*)

CIRCUS RINGMASTER: My! Your husband's getting heavy. You better tell him to lay off those imaginary cookies!

(*He empties the contents of the sack onto the floor. Rubber body parts—severed limbs, a flayed torso, bloody fingers, items that one could buy at any gag store—spill out onto the stage*)

(*The Circus Ringmaster steps away, revealing Pagliacci, the Clown's decapitated head. The applause track plays, Pagliacci's head speaks*)

PAGLIACCI'S HEAD: Honey, I'm home!

(*The Circus Ringmaster turns to leave*)

BRIGHELLA: Why don't you stay for dinner, Circus Ringmaster? I'm serving prime rib and a side of bread pudding.

CIRCUS RINGMASTER: You're serving what . . . ?! (*Brighella gives an exaggerated wink of the eye. At the same time, someone taps a triangle offstage. Ding!*) Ohhhh. You little trickster! That certainly sounds mouth watering. I'll tell you what. Why don't you pretend I'm joining you for dinner?

(*The Circus Ringmaster leaves and slams the door behind him. The cardboard wall topples over. Brighella catches it and pushes it back. She takes a step towards Pagliacci's head*)

BRIGHELLA: Tough day at work—(*The cardboard wall falls again. Brighella leans against the wall and tries to look natural, while holding up the entire house*) A-hem. Tough day at work, dear?

PAGLIACCI'S HEAD: They shot me out of the cannon today. I'LL MURDER THE SONS OF BITCHES! I'LL SMASH MY FACE IN THEIR LUNGS AND GO, "AAAAHHHH!"

BRIGHELLA: Now, now.

PAGLIACCI'S HEAD: Sorry. I let it slip. I need a hug. (*Brighella steps away from the wall. It starts to fall again. She leans against it*) What are you doing, standing all the way over there? Come over here and stand next to me.

BRIGHELLA: Uh . . . no.

PAGLIACCI'S HEAD: No? What do you mean, "no"! Why not?

(*Brighella pulls a slanted table over to her with her foot*)

BRIGHELLA: Why not? Because . . . I want you to come over here. That's right. Why do I always have to come to you? Why don't you come to me for once—

PAGLIACCI'S HEAD: What are you, blind? Look at me! I'm a decapitated head, for god's sake! (*Brighella props the slanted table against the wall and lays her plate of imaginary cookies on it. The plate slides off and breaks on the stage. A moment later, we hear the sound of a plate smashing. They both stare at the plate*) Light travels faster than sound.

BRIGHELLA: What?

PAGLIACCI'S HEAD: The plate. We see it smash first and then we hear it.

BRIGHELLA: Oh. That sounds reasonable. Doesn't it?

PAGLIACCI'S HEAD: Very reasonable indeed.

(*Brighella gathers up Pagliacci's body parts*)

BRIGHELLA: Why don't you let me put you to bed and give you a nice massage.

PAGLIACCI'S HEAD (*sniffles*): You go on ahead, pumpkin. I don't feel very attractive tonight.

(*A studio audience track plays, "Awwww!" Brighella, her arms full of body parts, pulls up a slanted chair beside Pagliacci's head and sits*)

BRIGHELLA: I'll tell you what—(*She slides off the slanted chair . . .*) Ahhh! (*She hits the floor, scattering body parts across the stage. The snare drummer accents her fall with a drum roll and cymbal smash! Brighella stares at the snare drummer as if she hadn't noticed him before. Unable to comprehend his presence, she quietly walks over to the window behind him* *and draws the curtain closed, covering the snare drummer up. She then carefully sits on the slanted chair, bracing herself by firmly anchoring her feet to the stage)* I'll tell you what. I'll go run a hot bath for you. In the meantime, you practice your jokes. And, if you're good enough, the Circus Ringmaster might just promote you to whiteface clown.

PAGLIACCI'S HEAD: Then I get to shoot the cannon instead of getting shot out.

BRIGHELLA (*squeezes his cheek*): That's right.

PAGLIACCI'S HEAD (*takes a deep breath*): A-hem. Did you hear about the cross-eyed teacher?

BRIGHELLA: No, I didn't hear about the cross-eyed teacher.

PAGLIACCI'S HEAD: She . . . she . . . I'LL GOUGE OUT THEIR EYE-BALLS AND FUCK THEIR EYE SOCKETS! AAAHHHHH!

(*Brighella slaps him across the face. He stops*)

BRIGHELLA: I believe you were talking about the cross-eyed teacher?

PAGLIACCI'S HEAD: She had no control over her pupils.

(*The drummer plays "ba-num-bum!" behind the curtain*)

BRIGHELLA: That's very funny.

PAGLIACCI'S HEAD: You think? I made it up myself.

BRIGHELLA: That's a genuine knee-slapper. (*We hear the sound of screeching tires, followed by the "beep beep!" of a car horn. A second bloodstained, burlap sack flies through the paper window and lands on the stage. A moment later, we hear the sound of shattering glass. Brighella looks out the rip in the paper window and waves*) Thank you, Mister Bus Driver! (*She turns away. An aluminum lunch pail flies through the window and lands on the stage with a clank! We hear the bus driver gun the engine . . . vroom vroom! . . . and peel out. Brighella empties the contents of the second bloody burlap sack onto the stage. More rubber body parts spill out*)

(*She steps away, revealing Rodrigo, the Clown's decapitated head*)

PAGLIACCI'S HEAD: Tough day at school, son?

RODRIGO'S HEAD: The kids at school ripped me apart on the playground.

PAGLIACCI'S HEAD: Does it hurt, kid?

RODRIGO'S HEAD: It hurt like a bitch. Then, I remembered. (*Like a mantra*) "My body parts are made out of rubber, my spirit is the only thing that's real."

BRIGHELLA (*sings*): "Jesus loves me, this I know . . ."

BRIGHELLA AND PAGLIACCI'S HEAD (*sing*): "For the Bible tells me so."

(*Brighella kneels down and puts her arms around both heads*)

BRIGHELLA/PAGLIACCI'S HEAD/RODRIGO'S HEAD (*sing*): "Yes, Jesus loves me. Yes, Jesus . . ."

PAGLIACCI'S HEAD: I'LL KILL THE COCKSUCKERS! I'LL RIP—

(*Brighella, without missing a beat in the song, slaps Pagliacci's head. He stops and resumes singing as if nothing happened*)

BRIGHELLA/PAGLIACCI'S HEAD/RODRIGO'S HEAD (*sing*): "Yes, Jesus loves me. The Bible tells me so."

RODRIGO'S HEAD: Hey, Dad! Let's play some ball, you and me! Whaddya'say?

PAGLIACCI'S HEAD: Sure, son! Why the hell not! Throw me a heater, bambino! Put'er there, right down the pipe!

RODRIGO'S HEAD: Uh . . . Dad?

PAGLIACCI'S HEAD: What?

RODRIGO'S HEAD: The ball's on the table.

PAGLIACCI'S HEAD: Well, go get it.

(*A moment of uncomfortable silence. Brighella jumps up*)

BRIGHELLA: I'll get it! (*She gets the baseball*) Let me throw the first pitch!

PAGLIACCI'S HEAD: Gee, I don't know. Baseball's a man's game. Whaddya think, son?

RODRIGO'S HEAD: We'll let you pitch, Mom. But just this once.

PAGLIACCI'S HEAD: You heard the man! Put'er there! Right down the pipe! Hey, batter, batter, batter . . .

(*Brighella winds up and pitches the ball. The ball hits Pagliacci in the face and rolls away. His nose begins to bleed. A moment of uncomfortable silence*)

BRIGHELLA: I know! Why don't you pretend to play ball!

PAGLIACCI'S HEAD: That's a good idea! Put'er there, bambino! (*To Rodrigo's head*) Hey, batter, batter, batter . . .

RODRIGO'S HEAD: I'm going into my wind-up. And I pitch the ball!

PAGLIACCI'S HEAD: Batter, batter . . . SWING and a miss!

(*Brighella jumps up and cheers. Lights out*)

INTERVIEW WITH MICHAEL CHUNG, *author of* The Friendly Neighborhood

What prompts you to write plays?

I have a desire to make intimate, meaningful connections with other people through communication or the sharing of personal experiences—and I don't think I'm unusual in that respect. I'm drawn to dramatic writing because it is a more specific means of communication than language.

Arthur Schopenhauer said that language is a set of symbols which stand for concepts, and a concept is a generalization of an experience or that which is commonly understood to represent a general kind of experience. If this is true, then in order for me to communicate through the medium of language a particular experience that I have, I must translate my experience into a concept. In other words, I must assign to it an existing concept which will represent it in the ensuing conversation. But this involves manipulating my experience to make it "fit" the concept—generalizing the content of my experience until it resembles the "general kind of experience" which is commonly understood to be that which is represented by the concept. And because a generalization of an experience can never be as detailed as the original experience, much of the specificity and therefore meaning of the original experience—perhaps, even much of what made the original experience worth sharing—is lost in the generalization.

Thus, what is being communicated in a conversation are not experiences—but mere shadows of them. A theatrical production, on the other hand, has the potential to be a far more specific and accurate means of communication than language. The theater offers so many different sets of symbols which an artist can use to fashion a representation of the experience he or she wishes to communicate—a representation that is far more detailed, rich, and subtle than that which he or she could create using language alone.

What was the most important event in your life as a writer?

Graduate school was very important to me, but I think I became a true writer only after I left NYU. A dramatic writer must have an appreciation for, and a knowledge of, dramatic structure, and NYU gave me those things. In my humble opinion, successful art is equal parts craft and creativity: the product of a disciplined imagination. And this goes hand in hand with my understanding of art as communication—and I like to use "communication" rather than "expression," because "communication" stresses the role of the audience in a way that "expression" does not. An artist *communicates* something to his audience; he makes a real connection with them. He doesn't just *express* himself—that sounds like getting something off your chest without regard for whether your audience understands you or not. And in order for your audience to understand you through the medium of your work, the work must be built upon a foundation of structural principles.

An illustration: writing a play or a screenplay is like writing a sentence. A sentence has an inner logic or principles which govern the relationships between words. Without them, the sentence would be gibberish, and the experience, for which the sentence is merely a vehicle, would be lost. The content of a play must also be governed by an inner logic for the same reasons. However, I'm *not* saying that the same inner logic should be used over and over. In fact, a writer should come up with his own inner logic. To a large extent, that's what it means to be creative or inventive.

How would you describe your work?

I think what I'm doing is called "expressionism," but I could be using the term incorrectly. I begin with an idea, and then I attempt to physicalize it or dramatize it. People have told me that that's a cold and impersonal way to approach playwriting; that I should be starting from experiences instead of ideas. But I think that opinion is the result of a misconception about the nature of ideas. An idea is an abstraction from meaningful experiences, the product of an attempt to discover what is common to them, what they are manifestations of, what it is that makes them seem "meaningful." So, if I wanted to be really specific, I too could say that I begin from experience. Furthermore, the communication of ideas doesn't have to be a dry and passionless affair. Look at Nietzsche. The thing I admire about Schopenhauer and Nietzsche is that they are both philosophers and artists. Schopenhauer will meticulously build an argument for pages, and then suddenly he'll crystallize it with a visual metaphor—he'll compare it to a body of water or to the cardboard scenery of a play. And then you'll think, "Ohhhh! I didn't know what the hell you were talking about before, but *now* I get it." Schopenhauer and Nietzsche have convinced me that art is the best way to communicate philosophical ideas.

Contributors

Daniel Aukin is the Artistic Director of Soho Repertory Theatre. Before that, he served as co-producer of the 4th "Summer Camp" festival. He is a founding member of Physical Plant Theater, based in Austin, Texas. At Soho Rep, Daniel has directed *The Year of the Baby* by Quincy Long, *Cat's-Paw* by Mac Wellman, and *A Phaedra Play* by Judy Elkan.

Neena Beber's plays include *Thirst, A Common Vision, Tomorrowland, The Brief But Exemplary Life of the Living Goddess*, and *Failure to Thrive*. She has received an Amblin Commission from Playwrights Horizons and an A.S.K. Exchange to the Royal Court. Her ten-minute play *Misreadings* was produced at ATL's Humana Festival and included in *Best American Short Plays: 1996–1997*. Short films: *Bad Dates,* based on her 1-act, *Food*. She has been an Associate Artist at the Magic Theatre and is a member of HB Playwrights Unit and New Dramatists. *Clock* is dedicated to Charles and Joyce Beber.

Lisa Burdige is a writer/director whose work has been seen at Yale Cabaret, La Mama Galleria, The Piano Store, and Soho Rep. Her fiction, poetry, and journalism have been published in national magazines. Grants and awards: James Michener Fellow, Analecta Best Short Story Award, NYU Fiction Fellowship.

Michael Chung graduated from Cornell University and has an MFA in dramatic writing from NYU's Tisch School of the Arts.

Dennis Davis is the author of *The Life of Violet, The Song of Seven Cities, Rough Trade: The Remnant Play and Other Works*. He resides in Washington Heights, New York City.

Dan Dzindzihashvili has had his plays produced in theaters throughout New York City including Soho Rep, Ensemble Studio Theatre, and HERE, as well as Immigrants' Theatre Project. As a producer, shows include Karen Finley's *The Return of the Chocolate-Smeared Woman* and *Herman Farrell's Bedfellows*, both directed by Jim Simpson for The Bat Theatre Company at the Flea. He studied playwriting with Tony Kushner, Irene Fornes, and Len Jenkins at NYU's Dramatic Writing Program, where he received his MFA. He is a Georgian born in Israel.

Jason T. Garrett holds an MFA in Dramatic Writing from NYU's Tisch School of the Arts, an MA in Dramatic Literature from the Catholic University of America, and a BA in English and Theatre from the University of Tennessee at Knoxville. Jason is Adjunct Faculty at the University of North Carolina at Charlotte and has also taught at NYU. Jason has had readings or productions of his plays at Expanded Arts (NYC), Soho Rep (NYC), the Schaeberle Studio (NYC), Tisch School of the Arts (NYC), Source Theatre (DC), the National Theatre (DC), Hartke Theatre (DC), the American College Theatre Festival (Most Promising Playwright, 1996), Clarence Brown Theatre Lab (TN), Oak Ridge Playhouse (TN), Louisiana Tech University, and the University of Tennessee. In Summer 2000, Jason received a grant from the Drama League to develop a one-woman show based on Charlotte Perkins Gilman's 1892 short story "The Yellow Wallpaper." This original adaptation was first produced on August 29, 2000, at the Schaeberle Studio in New York, NY, under the direction of Laura Hackman and starring Jacqueline Underwood. In his spare time, Jason works as a Senior Technical Writer for software research and development firms. For more information, stop by http://www.JasonTGarrett.com.

Mark Green has an MFA in dramatic writing from NYU. His works have been performed on stages in Washington, D.C. and New York City.

Emily Jenkins is the author of a book of cultural criticism, *Tongue First: Adventures in Physical Culture*, a children's novel, *The Secret Life of Billie's Uncle Myron*, and a picture book, *Five Creatures*. Her writing has appeared in *Glamour, Mademoiselle, Salon, Interview, Nerve, Feed,* and *The Village Voice*. Her only other play, *Animal Shelter*, was performed as part of the ten-minute festival in Soho Rep's Summer Camp 5. She has a doctorate in English Literature from Columbia.

Henry Kandel is a writer, director, and performer with a background in improvisational theater. He lives in Brooklyn with his wife and son, and teaches physics at Saint Ann's School. He founded the group Hybrid Vigor, which presents both written and improvised plays.

Madelyn Kent has directed her plays *Crawl* and *Burrow* for Soho Rep's Summer Camp 4 and 5. Her full-length plays include: *World War Two, I Love You, Black Milk,* and *Nomads*. She has an MFA from the Tisch School of the Arts in playwriting and screenwriting.

David Lindsay-Abaire is the author of several full-length plays, including *Fuddy Meers, A Devil Inside, Wonder of the World, Dotting & Dashing, Kimberly Akimbo,* and *A Shows of Hands*. His work has been produced in New

York and around the country at Manhattan Theatre Club, Soho Rep and Woolly Mammoth, among others. He has received commissions from South Coast Rep, Mosaic Entertainment, Dance Theater Workshop, and the Jerome Foundation, as well as awards from Primary Stages, the Berrilla Kerr Foundation, the Lincoln Center LeComte du Nouoy Fund and the Tennessee Williams Literary Festival. He is a proud member of New Dramatists, as well as the Dramatists Guild and the Writers Guild of America.

John Poglinco's plays have been produced at the Belmont Italian-American Playhouse, Playwright's Horizons, The Ohio Theatre, The Tenement Museum, The Interlude Theatre, and Pulse Ensemble Theatre. He teaches dramatic writing at NYU.

J.R. Riddick is the author of *Every 1 is Guilty until Proven Black, 45 RPM,* and *Cosmic Retribution.* He has worked steadily in downtown theater since 1993, and his plays have been seen at New York Theatre Workshop and at NYU's Tisch School of the Arts. He is also producing director of Transcendence Entertainment.

Lucy Thurber recently participated as a guest artist at Perseverance Theatre for *Desire Under the Elm* and *Moby Dick.* She is the author of five plays: *Where We're Born, Ashville, Innocence Is a Sin, Killers and Other Family* and *Stay. Killers and Other Family* was produced at Rattlestick Theater for the 2000/01 season and was a finalist for the Princess Grace Award. *Innocence Is a Sin* was read as part of the spring reading series *6 @ 6: Discovering the Next Generation* at Manhattan Theatre Club; and was also a finalist for the 1998 Eugene O'Neill Playwrights Conference. *Dinner*, a ten-minute play, was produced by Soho Rep as part of the 1998 Summer Camp Festival, at Ensemble Studio Theater during the Octoberfest 1998 and at the Young Blood One-Act Festival. *Where We're Born* was given a workshop production at The Playwrights' Collective. Lucy is the recipient of the 2000/01 Manhattan Theatre Club Playwriting Fellowship Award, and her plays have been workshopped at Ensemble Studio Theater, Manhattan Theatre Club, The New Group, Rattlestick Theater and The Echo Theater Company.

ML